Singing

to

God

Hymns
and Songs
1965 — 1995
by
Michael Perry

Code No. 1207

Hope Publishing Company
CAROL STREAM IL 60188

FOREWORD

Michael Arnold Perry is a high-profile, highly respected Vicar in the Anglican Church. In addition, he is a prolific hymnist who served for a number of years as secretary for Jubilate Hymns, Ltd., producers of **Hymns for Today's Church, Carols for Today, Church Family Worship, Come Rejoice!** and **Psalm Praise**.

For those in the United States who need labels attached to everything (and I am one of those creatures), it is necessary to look beyond such preconceived images or we will miss the real person. With all his many accomplishments, Michael is a very modest individual. He models his life after the Christ he serves. What you see is what you get, so let us look a bit closer at the person.

To my knowlege, he is the only clergyman in all of England whose Vicarage is patrolled by a somewhat ornery donkey named "Bossy." Michael is priest-in-charge of the Parishes of Shipbourne and Tonbridge in County Wells, with six pastors, and the usual number of challenges that accompany such responsibilities. With all these obligations he still finds the time to edit books such as **The Daily Bible, Prayers for the People, The Dramatised Bible, The Wedding Book,** and **Songs from the Psalms,** and to write some extraordinary hymn texts. This literary output is not just an avocation. It is an integral part of this very creative individual's life.

Michael Perry's hymn texts travel well. They are not stilted or mundane. They sing and sound just as good in Toledo as they do in Tonbridge. Thus, it should come as no surprise that his hymns have gained the same kind of popularity here in the United States that they have achieved in the United Kingdom.

It has been quite some time since we suggested that he consider producing a collection of hymns by Michael Perry. How pleased we are that this has now happened. Born in 1942 in wartime England, as hymnwriters go he is relatively a youngster. Hopefully, this is just the first volume of hymns from this delightful person and this promising resource.

George H. Shorney
March 1995

Available in the United Kingdom from:
Stainer & Bell Ltd.
P.O. Box 110, Victoria House
23 Gruneisen Road
Finchley, London N3 1DZ
Telephone: 0181-343 3303
Fax: 0181-343 3024

৬ক৬

Copyright permissions in the United Kingdom
are available from Jubilate Hymns Ltd.
Telephone: 0170-363 0038

৬ক৬

All of the hymn texts of Michael Perry are also available under
the CCL License Scheme.

Copyright permissions in the United States and Canada
are available from Hope Publishing Co., Carol Stream, IL 60188

৬ক৬

All of the hymn texts of Michael Perry are also available under
CCLI or the LicenSing programs.

৬ক৬

First Published in 1995
ISBN # 0-916642-59-3
Library of Congress Catalog Card Number 95-079497

Michael Perry

Information—The Author

Michael Arnold Perry was born on March 8, 1942 in Beckenham, Kent, England. He married Beatrice Mary Stott on 10th June 1967 in St. Helen's Parish Church, Lancashire. Their daughter Helen Mary, was born in 1969, and their son, Simon Mark, in 1973.

Michael was educated at Dulwich College, University College London, Oak Hill Theological College London, the University of Cambridge (Ridley Hall), and the University of Southampton. He obtained a Bachelor of Divinity (BD) degree in 1964, and a Master of Philosophy (MPhil) degree in 1973.

Ordained to the Church of England Ministry in the Diocese of Liverpool, Michael served as assistant curate at St. Helens Parish Church, Lancashire from 1965 to1968. He then moved as curate to Bitterne, Southampton and served from 1968 to 1972. In 1972 he was instituted as Vicar of Bitterne, in which post he remained until 1981.

From 1982, he became honorary Editorial Secretary and Company Secretary of Jubilate Hymns Ltd., a non-profit making company linked to a charitable trust. He remains a Director of that company, and a Trustee of the charity.

In 1981 he became Rector of Eversley, also in the Diocese of Winchester, and Chaplain/Lecturer, at the national Police Staff College, Bramshill, 1981-1987. He relinquished the Bramshill post in 1987 when a full-time Chaplain to the College was appointed to the College.

Michael was first elected to the General Synod, the governing body of the Church of England, in 1985, and again in 1994.

Michael was inducted as Vicar of Tonbridge in 1989. In 1993, he became Chairman of the Church Pastoral Aid Society.

In the list of publications by Jubilate members below, Michael's books are indicated *

Information—Life with the *Jubilate* Group

The *Jubilate* group, as it has come to be known, was founded in the early 1960's by Michael Baughen (who eventually became Rector of All Soul's, Langham Place in London, and then Anglican Bishop of Chester) and friends closely involved in work among young people. The group pooled their talents to meet the challenge of a new generation in the UK, who wished to extend their singing beyond the foursquare ways of metrical hymnody, and the unpredictability of Anglican chant!

Breaking new ground

Initially, no publisher could be found to support the first joint enterprise, *Youth Praise* (1966). The Church Pastoral Aid Society (a long-established English home missionary society under royal patronage) came to the rescue, later publishing *Youth Praise 2* (1969), and *Psalm Praise* (1973) which was a contemporary effort to revitalize the use of Psalms. *Youth Praise* was a best-seller in its time, and *Psalm Praise* because of its diversity broke new ground; eventually it was merged into *Psalms for Today* and *Songs from the Psalms* (see below).

As the work on *Psalm Praise* got under way, the group comprised Michael Baughen, Richard Bewes (who later succeeded him as Rector of All Souls), Christopher Collins, Timothy Dudley-Smith (to become Bishop of Thetford), Christopher Idle, Gavin Reid (to become Bishop of Maidstone), Edward Shirras (to become Archdeacon of Northolt), Michael Saward (to become Canon Treasurer of St. Paul's Cathedral), James Seddon, Norman Warren (to become Archdeacon of Rochester) and David Wilson and Michael Perry—a mixed bunch of talent, in terms of words and music.

Pioneering hymnal

In the mid-1970's, as an enlarged section of the group under Michael Baughen's leadership, we began to apply ourselves to the production of a pioneering modern language hymnal.[1] After years of conference and continuous application, *Hymns for Today's Church* was born in 1982. *HTC* now sells in six separate editions.

George Shorney of Hope Publishing in Carol Stream, Illinois, USA, had already enlisted the independent cooperation of Timothy Dudley-Smith, and then visited me in Eversley to secure the alliance of the extended *Jubilate Hymns* group. George's determined effort to recruit English hymn writers has resulted in a mutual enrichment of the USA and UK repertoires.[2] Thus *Jubilate* and their works have found their way into USA hymnals—*Worship, Rejoice in the Lord, The Hymnal 1982, Psalter Hymnal, The Worshiping Church, The Baptist Hymnal, Christian Worship, Trinity Hymnal* and many others. Similarly, many American hymns have emerged in *Jubilate* publications.

A mixture of styles

Jubilate authors and musicians—there are now forty of us—differ remarkably in our style, taste and approach. Since we are all friends, and can take firm criticism from one another, there is a considerable strength in our working together. Our breadth of style is also reflected in the variety of *Jubilate* publications: *Hymns for Today's Church: first edition*† (1982), *Hymns for Today's Church: second edition** (inclusive language, 1987),*Church Family Worship** (1986 and 1988), *Carols for Today** (1986), *Carol Praise* (1987), *Let's Praise!* (1988 and 1994), *The Wedding Book** (1989), *Psalms for Today** and *Songs from the Psalms** (1989-90), *Come Rejoice!** (1990), *Hymns for the People*† (1993), *World Praise*† (1993 and 1995). All these were published either by *Hodder & Stoughton* (to become *HodderHeadline*), or by *Marshall Pickering/HarperCollins*.

In addition, several of the *Jubilate* group have music publications in their own right, often with other publishers. In the list which follows, the volumes for which I was responsible as Editor (in every case with an editorial team, and certainly with competent musicians—because I am not one!)—are marked '*'. Where I was simply a words editor, the title above is marked '†'.

Filling the gaps
My role apart from being editor was often to fill the gaps. Especially with *Psalms for Today*, where a certain corpus of psalms needed to be covered and other writers were not always forthcoming in time—or they all chose Psalms 23 and 121! I disciplined myself to get harsh criticism where necessary, and always the detached approval of other writers before allowing myself to include my own work. I also had the problem that, however much I might put forward some author's versions, if no-one would write music to them, they could not be published. In fact, it had never been easy to satisfy critics with any of our books—since, each time, we were pioneering in directions few others had taken; alternatives were simply not available, so we had to innovate. Having said that, we used as widely as we could the offerings of other contemporary writers where appropriate. For instance we encouraged and cajoled the Catholic writer Brian Foley to write more of his striking and unusual Psalm versions.

Non-serious music
From time to time, and timorously, I have submitted a melody to my music editor friends. The pattern has normally been this: after months during which I have hear nothing, I call them to ask, "What happened to my tune", only to receive the reply, "I didn't think you were serious." There have been notable exceptions. But very few!

In 1965, after much inhaling as a student in Cambridge from a pot-pourri of 'pop' and abstruse classics I gained a little musical confidence. *Calypso Carol* was the outcome. It was written for the end-of-term concert at Oak Hill (theological) College in London, where I was also a student.

The inspiration for *Calypso* came from a chance remark—and a fairly artless one—by Peter Hancock, then curate at Christ Church Beckenham. In a Christmas address to young people, he asked, "How would *you* like to be born in a stable?". Hence, "See him lying on a bed of straw etc." Shortly after this, Peter was succeeded by *Jubilate* member Richard Bewes who enjoyed singing calypsos—mostly about cricket, or 'Liza'—to his guitar (unbeknown to us he was courting a girl in the congregation called Elizabeth; they eventually married.) Richard would write calypso's for every social event—welcome parties, farewell parties etc. I caught the disease from him, and proceeded to do the same throughout my student days. So Peter gave me the concept for *Calypso Carol*, and Richard gave me the medium.

Calypso Carol became popular through a technical accident. A luckless *BBC* engineer wiped out the tape of the Kings College Cambridge Carol Service in the days before it went out 'live'. This event was a national tradition, and listening to it was part of many people's Christmas. The *BBC* hastily rearranged a service of carols, using the singer Cliff Richard (a household name in England, though scarcely known in the USA) as a draw. He chose to sing, among other items *Calypso Carol*. It quickly became a 'standard' carol in the UK, and British Commonwealth countries. It was translated into German and Nordic languages. Only very recently has it begun to be published in North America. There are others, but I have hopes for one in particular: it is the tune called *Beatrice* after my lovely and long-suffering wife. It was first published in *Hymns for the People* (1993) and is set to the words which mean more to me than any other text of mine: *The hands of Christ.*

---

[1] See: *Hymns in Today's Language*, Christopher Idle, Grove Books, Bramcote, Nottingham, UK; 1982.

[2] See: *The Hymnal Explosion in North America*, George H Shorney, Hope Publishing Company, Carol Stream, Illinois 60188; 1988.

Information—List of Music/Worship Publications
by *Jubilate Hymns* and *Jubilate* Artists

Books prior to 1995

Youth Praise (1 & 2), Falcon—Hymns and songs selection for youth work—seven formats (1966 & 1969). See also: *Let's Praise!*

Psalm Praise, Falcon/Kingsway—Psalm versions selection for worship—Three formats: Music and words, Case bound Words only, Limp Words only (1973). See also: *Psalms for Today, Songs from the Psalms*

Jesus Praise, Scripture Union—Song selection for general use—Several formats including Hardback and Spiral back Music and Words, Limp Words only (1982)

Caroling*, Marshall Pickering/HarperCollins—A popular selection from Carol Praise. Words Booklet) (1989)

Anglican Praise, Oxford University Press—A collection of Modern Hymns supplemental to *The Anglican Hymn Book*. Two formats: Music Edition, Words Edition (1987)

The Wedding Book*, Marshall Pickering/HarperCollins—Music and Words Case bound, Limp Words (1989)

Prom Praise Solos, Marshall Pickering/HarperCollins—Music and Words Limp (1989)

Come Rejoice!* Marshall Pickering/HarperCollins/Hope Publishing Company, USA—Two formats: Music and Words Limp, Words Limp (1989)

Current Books

Hymns for Today's Church, Hodder & Stoughton (First Edition)—Two formats: Words, Music and Words (1981)

Hymns for Today's Church, Hodder & Stoughton (Second Edition*)—Five formats: Double column Words, Hardback Words edition, Music and Words, Melody and Words, Giant Print (1987/8)

Church Family Worship*, Hodder & Stoughton—Three formats: Case bound Words only (1986—now discontinued in this format), Music and Words (1988), Small Limp Words (1989)

Carols for Today*, Hodder & Stoughton—Three formats: Words only, Music and Words Case bound, Music and Words Limp (1986/7)
Carols for Today Supplement Hodder & Stoughton—Music Limp (1990)

Carol Praise*, Marshall Pickering/HarperCollins—Two editions: Limp Music and Words, Words only (1987)

Play Carol Praise, A Christmas Selection for Instruments Marshall Pickering/HarperCollins—Music Limp 1990

Let's Praise! The Worship Songbook for a New Generation Marshall Pickering/HarperCollins—Two formats: Music and Words Case bound, Words Edition Limp (1988)

Let's Praise! 2 Marshall Pickering/HarperCollins, Music and Words edition Hardback (1994)

Let's Praise! 1 and 2 Combined Words edition, Limp (1994)

The Dramatized Bible*, Marshall Pickering/HarperCollins and The Bible Society—Case bound (1989)

Psalms for Today*, Hodder & Stoughton—Music and Words Edition—Two formats: Case bound and Spiral bound (1990)

Songs from the Psalms*, Hodder & Stoughton—Music and Words Edition—Two formats: Case bound and Spiral bound (1990)

Psalms for Today and Songs from the Psalms*, Hodder & Stoughton: Combined Words edition (1990)

Dramatized Bible Readings for Festivals*, Marshall Pickering/HarperCollins and The Bible Society—Limp, (1991)

Prayers for the People*, Marshall Pickering/HarperCollins—Two editions: Minister's Edition, People's Edition (1992)

Bible Praying*, HarperCollins—Fount Paperback (1992)

Lollipops, Fifty Easy Pieces for Organ Marshall Pickering/HarperCollins (1990)

Hymns for the People, Marshall Pickering/HarperCollins—(Inclusive hymn book in contemporary musical arrangement) Two editions: Case bound, Music and Words, Limp Words only (1993)

World Praise, Marshall Pickering/HarperCollins, Limp, Music and Words edition and Words Booklets (1993, 1995)

Responsorial Psalms, Marshall Pickering/HarperCollins, Hardback Music and Words (1994)

Preparing for Worship*, HarperCollins 1995

Sing Mission Praise, HarperCollins 1995 ?

Acknowledgments

My publishers—especially George Shorney and his
colleagues at *Hope*

My mentors—especially Timothy Dudley-Smith and
Christopher Idle

My family—especially my wife, Beatrice

My assistants—especially Bunty and Valerie

My fellow editors and arrangers—especially
David Iliff, David Peacock, Noël Tredinnick and
Norman Warren,

Michael Perry

*Tune names at the foot of each hymn or song indicate
melodies to which they were first published in the UK. I
am equally grateful to other composers who have set
my words, but whose names are not recorded.*

*The listed tunes are not intended to be
definitive—especially not to prevent interested
musicians from creating new music to carry the words.*

*Those intending publication should seek the permission
of Hope Publishing Company or of Jubilate Hymns Ltd.*

Contents

1.

A child is born in Bethlehem,
    Sing nowell!
the royal flower to David's stem.
    Alleluia, alleluia!

Sing praises through the whole wide earth,
    Sing nowell!
for Mary gives the Savior birth.
    Alleluia, alleluia!

He lies within a manger bare,
    Sing nowell!
and shepherds kneel to worship there.
    Alleluia, alleluia!

He comes to be our hope of peace,
    Sing nowell!
to bring imprisoned souls release.
    Alleluia, alleluia!

Our guilt has found a certain cure,
    Sing nowell!
for Christ makes our salvation sure.
    Alleluia, alleluia!

Tunes: A child is born/Norman Warren, Sing nowell/16th Century German melody—8.3.8.8.

2.

All heaven rings with joyful songs
as angels tell the story
of one who comes to right our wrongs
and take us up to glory.

The silent earth is filled with awe
and mortal men stand trembling;
for God is found among the poor,
our very selves resembling.

The Lord is born this holy day
of Mary, virgin mother;
God's child of grace, love's perfect way,
our savior and our brother.

Come, Christians, greet the living Word,
ascribing truth and merit;
let heaven and earth with one accord
praise Father, Son and Spirit!

Tune: Barbara Allen/English traditional—8.7.8.7. iambic

3.

All who are thirsty, come to the Lord,
all who are hungry, feed on his word;
buy without paying food without price,
eat with thanksgiving God's sacrifice.

Why spend your money, yet have no bread;
why work for nothing? Trust God instead!
He will provide you richest of food:
come to the waters, drink what is good.

Call on God's mercy while he is near,
turn from your evil, come without fear;
ask him for pardon—grace will abound!
This is the moment he can be found.

Where once were briers, flowers will grow,
where lives were barren, rivers will flow:
praise to our Savior, grace and renown—
ours is the blessing, his be the crown!

From Isaiah 55.
Copyright © 1993 by Michael Perry/Jubilate Hymns Ltd.;
USA © 1993 by Hope Publishing Company, Carol Stream, IL 60188.

Tune: by Mutya Lopez Solis—5.4.5.4.D.

4.

Angels, praise him,
heavens, praise him,
waters, praise him,
  Alleluia!
creatures of the Lord,
all praise him
  for evermore:

Sun, praise him,
moon, praise him,
stars, praise him,
  Alleluia!
showers, praise him,
dews, praise him
  for evermore:

WOMEN
  Wind, praise him,
  fire, praise him,
  heat, praise him,
    Alleluia!
  winter, praise him,
  summer, praise him
    for evermore:

MEN
  Nights, praise him,
  days, praise him,
  light, praise him,
    Alleluia!
  lightnings, praise him,
  clouds, praise him,
    for evermore:

WOMEN
Earth, praise him,
mountains, praise him,
hills, praise him,
  Alleluia!
green things, praise him,
wells, praise him
  for evermore:

MEN
Seas, praise him,
rivers, praise him,
fish, praise him,
  Alleluia!
birds, praise him,
beasts, praise him
  for evermore:

Nations, praise him,
churches, praise him,
saints, praise him,
  Alleluia!
all his people,
join to praise him
  for evermore!

5.

As we walk along beside you,
and we hear you speak of mercy,
then it seems our hearts are burning
for we find you in the sharing of the word.

As we ask that you stay with us
and we watch what you are doing,
then our eyes begin to open
for we see you in the breaking of the bread.

As we reach for you believing
and we go to love and serve you,
then our lives will be proclaiming
that we know you in the rising from the dead.

From Luke 24.
Copyright © 1982 by Michael Perry/Jubilate Hymns Ltd.;
USA © 1982 by Hope Publishing Company, Carol Stream, IL 60188.

Tune: Burning Heart/Norman Warren—8.8.8.11.

6.

Babylon
  by the rivers of sorrow!
Hang your harps
  by the old willow tree.
All our joy is gone,
  there's no hope for tomorrow.
We'll never forget you,
  O Jerusalem!

'Sing', they say,
  'all the songs of your city!'
How shall we sing
  in an alien land?—
captives brought away
  without mercy or pity!
We'll never forget you,
  O Jerusalem!

Glory be
  to the name of the Father:
glory be
  for the grace of the Son;
glory be
  in the joy of the Spirit:
we look for the mercy
  of the Three-in-One!

From Psalm 137.
Copyright © 1990 by Michael Perry/Jubilate Hymns Ltd.;
USA © 1990 by Hope Publishing Company, Carol Stream, IL 60188.

Tune: Summertime/G Gershwin (1898-1937)—Irregular

7.

Be gracious to me, Lord,
and hold my spirit fast,
that I may shelter by your side
until the storm is past.

Though snares are set for me,
yet I will sleep in peace,
for I have asked the care of God
whose love shall never cease.

My soul, awake and sing—
such boundless love recall,
exalt God's name above the skies,
God's glory over all!

From Psalm 57.
Copyright © 1973 by Michael Perry/Jubilate Hymns Ltd.;
USA © 1983 by Hope Publishing Company, Carol Stream, IL 60188.

Tune: Saigon/Norman Warren, Holyrood/ J Watson (1816-1880);
Boundless Love/Norman Warren—S.M. (6.6.8.6.)

8.

Bethlehem, the chosen city of our God,
where the stem of faithful Jesse duly flowered:
there Messiah in a manger humbly lay,
born of Mary, born for us on Christmas Day!

Israel's land would suffer much in grief and pain
till the hand of God should touch the earth again;
then the royal star of Jacob would arise,
David's scepter soon appear before their eyes.

Judah's hills their age-long vigil silent kept,
God fulfilled the pledge while Israel sullen slept;
only shepherds watching bravely through the night
found their Shepherd, stooped to see the infant light.

Bethlehem, the chosen city of our God,
where the stem of faithful Jesse duly flowered:
there Messiah in a manger humbly lay,
born of Mary, born for us on Christmas Day!

Tune: Pieds en l'air/Peter Warlock (1894-1930)
or Bethlehem/Norman Warren—11.11.11.11.

9.

Bethlehem, what greater city
can in fame with you compare?
For the gracious God of heaven
chose to meet our people there.

Was there ever beauty brighter
than the star which shone that night
to proclaim the incarnation
of our God, the world's true light?

From the East come men of learning,
rich the treasures that they hold—
tributes to a greater wisdom,
gifts of incense, myrrh and gold.

Sacrifice, redeemer, savior!
Incense shows that God has come,
gold, our mighty king proclaims him,
myrrh foretells his silent tomb.

Jesus Christ, to you be glory,
Lord of lords whom we adore
with the Father and the Spirit:
God be praised for evermore!

After Prudentius (348-c.413).
Copyright © 1986 by Michael Perry/Jubilate Hymns Ltd.;
USA © 1986 by Hope Publishing Company, Carol Stream, IL 60188.

Tune: Stuttgart/C F Witt (1660-1716)/Descant: David Iliff—8.7.8.7.

10.

Blest be the God of Israel
      who comes to set us free;
who visits and redeems us,
      who grants us liberty.
The prophets spoke of mercy,
      of rescue and release:
God shall fulfill the promise
      to bring the gift of peace.

Now from the house of David
      a child of grace has come;
a savior who will lead us
      to our eternal home.
Before him goes his herald,
      forerunner in the way,
the prophet of salvation,
      the messenger of Day.

On those who live in darkness
      the sun begins to rise—
the dawning of forgiveness
      upon the sinner's eyes;
to guide the feet of pilgrims
      along the paths of peace:
O bless our God and Savior,
      with songs that never cease!

From Luke 1/Benedictus.
(See also 'O bless the God of Israel')
Copyright © 1973 by Michael Perry/Jubilate Hymns Ltd.;
USA © 1973 by Hope Publishing Company, Carol Stream, IL 60188.

Tune: Merle's tune or Morning Light/G J Webb (1803-1887)
or Roewen/Roger Mayor—7.6.7.6.D.

11.

Blow upon the trumpet!
Clap your hands together,
sound aloud the praises of the Lord your king.
He has kept his promise,
granting us salvation:
let his people jubilantly shout and sing!

Blow upon the trumpet!
Let the nations tremble;
see his power obliterate the sun and moon.
This is God's own army
bringing all to judgment,
for the day of Jesus Christ is coming soon.

Blow upon the trumpet!
Arrows in the lightening
fly the storm of battle where he marches on.
Glory to our shepherd
keeping us through danger,
setting us like jewels in his royal crown!

Blow upon the trumpet!
Christ is surely coming,
heaven's forces mobilizing at his word.
We shall rise to meet him;
death at last is conquered,
God gives us the victory
   through Christ our Lord!

From Psalm 95, Joel 2 etc.
Copyright © 1982 by Michael Perry/Jubilate Hymns Ltd.;
USA © 1982 by Hope Publishing Company, Carol Stream, IL 60188.

Tune: Philip James/Norman Warren—6.6.11.D.

12.

Born as a stranger,
laid in a manger,
  Jesus, the Lord of heaven and earth;
to us descending,
sinners befriending,
  bring us to glory by your birth!

Infant so tender!
Gone is the splendor,
  Jesus, that graced your Father's home;
our nature wearing,
our sorrows bearing,
  poor and alone for us you come.

Lord of all lowliness,
perfect in holiness,
  Jesus the Christ, of whom we sing;
we bow before you,
praise and adore you:
  be our true savior and our king!

Tune: Schonster Herr Jesu/*Silesian Folk Songs* Leipzig (1842); Ginette/Paul
Whitell—5.5.8.D.

13.

Born of the water,
born of the Spirit—
   called by the wind and the fire;
sealed with the promise,
we shall inherit
   more than the most we desire.

One through redemption,
one with the Father—
   children of grace and of heaven;
joyfully sharing
faith with each other,
   sinners whose sins are forgiven.

Glory, all glory,
glory to Jesus—
   die we in him and we live!
friends in his service,
heirs to the treasures
   God, and God only, can give.

Tune: Born of the water/Christopher Norton,
Passfield/Simon Beckley—5.5.7.7.D.

14.
Bring to the Lord a glad new song,
children of grace extol your king:
your love and praise to God belong—
to instruments of music, sing!
Let those be warned who spurn God's name,
let rulers all obey God's word,
for justice shall bring tyrants shame—
let every creature praise the Lord!

Sing praise within these hallowed walls,
worship beneath the dome of heaven;
by cymbals' sounds and trumpets' calls
let praises fit for God be given:
with strings and brass and wind rejoice—
then, join our song in full accord
all living things with breath and voice;
let every creature praise the Lord!

From Psalms 149 and 150.
Copyright © 1982 by Michael Perry/Jubilate Hymns Ltd.;
USA © 1982 by Hope Publishing Company, Carol Stream, IL 60188.

Tune: Jerusalem/C H H Parry (1848-1918)—D.L.M. (8.8.8.8.D.)

15.

By flowing waters of Babylon
we hung our harps on the willows:
how shall we sing our Jehovah's song
    in a foreign land, far away?

They who oppress us and mock our grief
tell us to sing and be merry:
how can we worship when spirits fail
    in an alien land, far away?

If we forget you, Jerusalem,
may we keep silence for ever!
Still we remember our distant home
    in another land, far away.

From Psalm 137
Copyright © 1973 by Michael Perry/Jubilate Hymns Ltd.;
USA © 1973 by Hope Publishing Company, Carol Stream, IL 60188.

Tune: Solent Breezes/Michael Perry—9.8.9.8.

16.

By rivers of sorrow we sat and remembered
the city of happiness where we belong;
our harps and our melodies hung in the branches,
and there our tormentors demanded a song!

WOMEN

O how shall we sing in the anguish of exile—
the songs of the Lord in a far away land?
Jerusalem, see if I ever forget you
till death take my voice and the skill of my hand!

MEN

You daughter of Babylon, doomed to destruction,
you people of Edom who throw down our walls,
be warned of the judgment on you and your children
when blasphemy fails and when tyranny falls.

And then shall the strings of the harp yield their music,
and then shall the tune of our song be restored;
and then shall the powers of the earth see the purpose,
the strong, the unquenchable, love of the Lord.

Tune: Streets of Laredo/American traditional—12.11.12.11.

17.
Child in a stable:
how lovely is this place
    where God is able
to show such perfect grace!
No princely babe that smiled
or palace that beguiled,
in history or fable,
could ever match this Child
    within a stable.

God comes in weakness,
and to our world for love
    descends with meekness
from realms of light above.
This Child shall heal our wrong,
for sorrow give a song,
and hope in place of bleakness;
for nothing is so strong
    as God in weakness.

Now night is ended!
The chasm that divides
    at last is mended,
and God with us abides.
For on this happy morn
new glory wakes the dawn;
the Sun is high ascended—
to us a Child is born,
    and night is ended!

After E Flechier (1632-1710).
Copyright © 1986 by Michael Perry/Jubilate Hymns Ltd.;
USA © 1986 by Hope Publishing Company, Carol Stream, IL 60188.

Tune: Dans cette étable/French traditional melody—5.11.6.6.7.11.

18.

Child of gladness, child of sorrow,
crib today but cross tomorrow;
holy Child who comes to borrow
   peasant robe and stable bare:

Child as all our children tender,
prince removed from heaven's splendor:
wealth and glory you surrender
   all our bitter pain to share.

Child in Bethlehem appearing,
neither hurt nor hatred fearing:
you we worship, God revering,
   Jesus, Savior, hear our prayer.

Tunes: Old Yeavering/Noël Tredinnick, Quem pastores laudavere/14th Century German
carol melody—8.8.8.7.

19.

Child of heaven born on earth—
let the music sound his praises:
Child of heaven born on earth—
sing to greet the savior's birth!

Christ, our hope, our joy, appears—
for this time we have been waiting;
Christ our hope, our joy appears—
promise of a thousand years.
    Child of heaven . . .

Cold within a lowly cave,
lightly wrapped, in manger lying;
cold within a lowly cave
is our God who stoops to save.
    Child of heaven . . .

Jesus, king and mighty One,
gentle babe in Mary's keeping;
Jesus, king and mighty One,
come to make our hearts your throne!
    Child of heaven . . .

From the French.
Copyright © 1986 by Michael Perry/Jubilate Hymns Ltd.;
USA © 1986 by Hope Publishing Company, Carol Stream, IL 60188.

Tune: Il est né/French traditional melody—7.8.7.7

20.

Christ is born to be our king—
listen, as the angels sing,
to the heavens echoing,
   'Glory be to God on high!'

Shepherds in the fields at night
hear the tidings, see the light,
find the child, in praise unite:
   'Glory be to God on high!'

Christians down the ages tell
Christ can break the powers of hell,
so that we may sing as well,
   'Glory be to God on high!'

Tune: Christ is born/David Sanderson—7.7.7.7.

21.
Christ is born within a stable:
greet the day when heaven smiled!
Shepherds, fast as they are able,
run to see the holy Child.
 Alleluia, alleluia,
 alleluia! Amen.

Eastern skies are brightly shining,
hope has come upon the earth;
angel songs with ours combining
tell the world of Jesus' birth.
 Alleluia, alleluia,
 alleluia! Amen.

Peal the bells and set them ringing,
spread the joyful news abroad;
come with faith and join our singing
to acclaim the incarnate Lord!
 Alleluia, alleluia,
 alleluia! Amen.

Tune: Russian Air/Russian traditional, descant: David Iliff—8.7.8.7.8.6.

22.

Christ is king! Our God has spoken:
'Sit beside me on my throne
till the reign of sin is broken,
till the righteous cause is won.'

Hear the promise of God's favour—
he will never take it back:
'You shall be a priest for ever
as the great Melchizedek'!

For the truth the Lord is fighting;
by his judgment tyrants fall:
right upholding, wrong requiting,
he will overcome them all.

Bright like dew at early morning,
weapons gleam from every hill;
all await the trumpet's warning
and obey the royal will.

Fierce the warfare, fraught with danger;
arrows fly and spears are hurled:
who can stand before God's anger
when he comes to judge the world?

Christ is king—the battle glorious!
Spread the victor's name abroad—
raised up high, enthoned, victorious:
praise him, praise the Son of God!

From Psalm 110.
Copyright © 1986 by Michael Perry/Jubilate Hymns Ltd.;
USA © 1986 by Hope Publishing Company, Carol Stream, IL 60188.

Tune: All for Jesus/J Stainer (1840-1901)—8.7.8.7.

23.

Christians, make a joyful sound,
sing to all the world around:
he is in a manger found,
the holy one, the infant son of Mary.
    Let the people join to say
    that Christ the Lord is born today,
    till the very earth shall raise
    the song of praise:
    'Nowell, nowell—
    Christ is born, the infant son of Mary!'

Mighty God, Emmanuel—
prince of whom the prophets tell,
child announced by Gabriel,
the holy one, the infant son of Mary.
    Let the people . . .

Come, you choirs, with gladness sing,
instruments of music bring—
eager to proclaim the king,
the holy One, the infant son of Mary.
    Let the people . . .

Love is here to seek and save—
heaven's master as a slave:
God so loved the world he gave
the holy One, the infant son of Mary.
    Let the people . . .

From the Latin.
Copyright © 1986 by Michael Perry/Jubilate Hymns Ltd.;
USA © 1986 by Hope Publishing Company, Carol Stream, IL 60188.

Tune: Resonet in laudibus (i)/14th Century German melody—Unique

24.

Come and hear the joyful singing,
  Alleluia, gloria,
set the bells of heaven ringing:
  alleluia, gloria,
God the Lord has shown us favor—
  alleluia, gloria,
Christ is born to be our savior.
  alleluia, gloria!

Angels of his birth are telling,
  Alleluia, gloria,
prince of peace all powers excelling;
  alleluia, gloria,
death and hell cannot defeat him:
  alleluia, gloria,
go to Bethlehem and greet him.
  alleluia, gloria!

Choir and people, shout in wonder,
  Alleluia, gloria,
let the merry organ thunder;
  alleluia, gloria,
thank our God for love amazing,
  alleluia, gloria,
Father, Son and Spirit praising.
  alleluia, gloria!

Tune: Nos Galan/Welsh traditional melody—8.7.8.7.D.

25.

Come and praise the Lord our king,	Alleluia,
let the world with carols ring.	alleluia!
Hear the news the angels tell,	Alleluia,
Christ is born, and all is well,	alleluia!
With the shepherds make your way,	Alleluia,
find the son of God today.	alleluia!
See the gifts the wise men hold—	Alleluia,
they bring incense, myrrh and gold.	alleluia!
In our praises take your part,	Alleluia,
thank him with a joyful heart.	alleluia!
Come and praise the Lord our king,	Alleluia,
let the world with carols ring.	alleluia!

Tune: Michael, row the boat/English traditional melody—7.4.7.4.

26.

Come and sing the Christmas story
    this holy night!
Christ is born: the hope of glory
    dawns on our sight.
Alleluia! Earth is ringing
with a thousand angels singing—
hear the message they are bringing
    this holy night.

Jesus, Savior, child of Mary
    this holy night,
in a world confused and weary
    you are our light.
God is in a manger lying,
self effacing, wealth denying,
life embracing, death defying
    this holy night.

Lord of all! Let us acclaim him
    this holy night;
king of our salvation name him,
    throned in the height,
Son of Man—let us adore him:
all the earth is waiting for him;
Son of God—we bow before him
    this holy night.

Tune: All through the night/Welsh traditional melody—8.4.8.4.8.8.8.4.

27.

Come, join to praise our God and king,
  his glories all-excelling:
the heavenly hosts his wonders sing,
  his mercies we are telling!
His arm is stronger than the sea—
  he calms its fitful anger;
he comes to set his people free,
  and rescues us from danger.

For all who trust his saving name
  are happy in believing;
they know his presence every day,
  his kindnesses receiving.
His kingdom stands on righteousness,
  with justice as foundation:
so praise our God, our victory,
  our song, our celebration!

From Psalm 89
Copyright © 1986 by Michael Perry/Jubilate Hymns Ltd.;
USA © 1986 by Hope Publishing Company, Carol Stream, IL 60188.

Tune: Golden Sheaves/A Sullivan (1842-1900)—8.7.8.7.D.

28.
Come, sing praises to the Lord above,
rock of our salvation, Lord of love;
with delight into God's presence move,
for the Lord our God is king!
  God is king above the mountains high,
  the ocean deep, the land and sky;
  mighty continents and islands lie
  within the hollow of God's hand.

Come to worship him and bow the knee,
praise our shepherd with humility;
humble creatures in his hand are we—
sing the praise of God the king!
  God is king . . .

Hear the story of God's people now,
you with stubborn hearts
    who will not bow;
learn what happened long ago and how
God can show you who is king!
  God is king . . .

Forty years God kept the prize away,
made them wander
    till they would obey,
exiled all of them until the day
they would honor God as king:
  Gods is king . . .

From Psalm 95/Venite (UK version has slight variants)
Copyright © 1973 by Michael Perry/Jubilate Hymns Ltd.;
USA © 1973 by Hope Publishing Company, Carol Stream, IL 60188.

Tune: Calypso Carol/Michael Perry—Irregular

29.
Come, worship God
    who is worthy of honor,
enter his presence
    with thanks and a song!
He is the rock of his people's salvation,
to whom our jubilant praises belong.

Ruled by his might
    are the heights of the mountains,
held in his hands
    are the depths of the earth;
his is the sea, his the land,
    for he made them,
king above all gods,
    who gave us our birth.

We are his people,
    the sheep of his pasture,
he is our maker and to him we pray;
gladly we kneel
    in obedience before him—
great is the God
    whom we worship this day!

Now let us listen,
    for God speaks among us;
open our hearts
    and receive what he says:
peace be to all
    who remember his goodness,
trust in his word and rejoice in his ways!

From Psalm 95/Venite.
Copyright © 1980 by Michael Perry/Jubilate Hymns Ltd.;
USA © 1980 by Hope Publishing Company, Carol Stream, IL 60188.

Tune: Epiphany Hymn/J. F. Thrupp (1827-1867)—11.10.11.10.

30.

Comes Mary to the grave;
no singing bird has spoken,
nor has the world awoken,
and in her grief all love lies lost
        and broken.

Says Jesus at her side,
no longer Jesus dying,
'Why, Mary, are you crying?'
She turns, with joy, 'My Lord! My love!'
        replying.

With Mary on this day
we join our voices praising
the God of Jesus' raising,
and sing the triumph of that love
        amazing.

From John 20.
Copyright © 1980 by Michael Perry/Jubilate Hymns Ltd.;
USA © 1980 by Hope Publishing Company, Carol Stream, IL 60188.

Tune: Easter Morning/Norman Warren or Church Close/David Iliff or Paschal
Dawn/John Barnard—6.7.7.11.

31.

Commit your way to God the Lord—
your cause will shine as bright as fire;
delight to do God's holy word
and you shall find what you desire.

Be still before the Lord and wait,
and do not fret when wrong succeeds;
refrain from anger, turn from hate,
for God will punish evil deeds.

Salvation comes from God alone:
the faithful know their help is sure;
to heaven all our needs are known,
and in God's strength we are secure.

Commit your way to God the Lord,
to peace and truth and grace aspire;
then mercy shall be your reward,
God's promises your heart's desire.

From Psalm 37.
Copyright © 1989 by Michael Perry/Jubilate Hymns Ltd.;
USA © 1989 by Hope Publishing Company, Carol Stream, IL 60188.

Tune: Summercourt/English melody—L.M. (8.8.8.8.)

32.

Creator of the stars of light,
our Lord of mercy and of might,
the Christ, redeemer of us all:
O hear your people when they call.

Through you, the savior crucified,
the guilty age of death has died;
you took our frail humanity
and gave the world its remedy:

And in the evening of our day
you rose to drive the shades away;
from Mary's honored virgin womb
you came, to take your people home.

The sun returning to the west,
the moon in pallid splendor dressed,
the glittering stars that pierce the skies,
obedient, keep their boundaries.

The unseen worlds below, above,
at your supreme direction move;
soon every creature of your hand
shall bow to your divine command.

We plead with you, our judge and Lord,
to come according to your word;
and in the hour of destiny
to save us from our enemy.

Now to the Father, with the Son
and Holy Spirit, Three-in-One;
to God whom heaven and earth adore
be praise and glory evermore! Amen.

From the Latin.
Copyright © 1986 by Michael Perry/Jubilate Hymns Ltd.;
USA © 1986 by Hope Publishing Company, Carol Stream, IL 60188.

Tune: Conditor alme siderum/Mode 4 melody—L.M. (8.8.8.8.)

33.
Down from the height of his glory he came,
willingly leaving his rightful domain:
Jesus was born in the image of man,
love was his motive and mercy his aim.

All through those days
   his resolve was the same—
Jesus the servant, the sharer of pain:
perfect obedience, the path of disdain,
down to a death of derision and shame.

Now God has granted him honor and fame,
taken him up to the highest to reign:
'Jesus is Lord!' every voice shall maintain,
all of creation shall bow to his name.

From Philippians 2 /The Song of Christ's Glory.
Copyright © 1986 by Michael Perry/Jubilate Hymns Ltd.;
USA © 1986 by Hope Publishing Company, Carol Stream, IL 60188.

Tunes: Purpose/Noël Tredinnick, Slane/Irish traditional melody—10.10.10.10.

34.

'Fear not, for I bring all people
good news of joy, good news of joy,
  good news of joy:

'On this day in David's city
Jesus is born, Jesus is born,
  Jesus is born.

'Glory in the highest heaven,
peace on the earth, peace on the earth,
  peace on the earth!'

From Luke 2.
Copyright © 1987 by Michael Perry/Jubilate Hymns Ltd.;
USA © 1987 by Hope Publishing Company, Carol Stream, IL 60188.

Tune: Come into his presence/Source unknown—8.4.4.4.

35.

    Fling wide the gates,
    unbar the ancient doors;
    salute your king
    in his triumphant cause!

Now all the world belongs to Christ our Lord:
let all creation greet the living Word!
    Fling wide . . .

Who has the right to worship him today?
All those who gladly serve him and obey.
    Fling wide . . .

He comes to save all those who trust his name,
and will declare them free from guilt and shame.
    Fling wide . . .

Who is the victor glorious from the fight?
He is our king, our life, our Lord, our right!
    Fling wide . . .

From Psalm 24.
Copyright © 1986 by Michael Perry/Jubilate Hymns Ltd.;
USA © 1986 by Hope Publishing Company, Carol Stream, IL 60188.

Tune: Crucifer/S. H. Nicholson (1875-1947)—10.10.Ref.

36.

Food to pilgrims given,
    strength upon the way;
Bread come down from heaven—
    Christ is ours today!
Feed us now, O Lord
    with this holy food—
  let your kingdom come, O Lord,
  let your kingdom come;
  let your kingdom come, O Lord,
  let your kingdom come.

Streams of grace are flowing—
    life from death for me;
truth and goodness growing
    for eternity.
Cleanse my soul, O Lord,
    with your precious blood—
  let your will be done, O Lord,
  let your will be done;
  let your will be done, O Lord,
  let your will be done.

I receive your blessing—
    Jesus, king divine;
all your love confessing
    in this bread and wine.
Send me out, O Lord,
    holy pure and good,
  till the world is won, O Lord,
  till the world is won;
  till the world is won, O Lord,
  till the world is won.

After Geonyong Lee
Copyright © 1995 by Michael Perry/Jubilate Hymns Ltd.;
USA © 1995 by Hope Publishing Company, Carol Stream, IL 60188.

Tune: Korean melody/possibly by Geonyong Lee—Unique

37.

'From heaven above I come to bring
the joyful news of Christ your king:
the holy infant born tonight
shall be your hope and your delight.

'For faithful is the prophets' word—
God sends to you this mighty Lord
to free you from your sin and shame;
the savior, Jesus, is his name.

'The One by whom the world was made
is in a humble manger laid;
and he to whom the throne was given
now stoops to raise you up to heaven.'

So with the shepherds make your way,
and find in Bethlehem today
the child of peace, the ever-blessed,
your master and your gracious guest:

Then bear the news that angels tell
to all the weary world as well;
let human power and pomp and pride
be vanquished at this Christmastide.

Sing praises to the Father, Son
and Holy Spirit—Three in One;
let God made known in Christ our Lord
be worshipped, honored, and adored!

After Martin Luther (1483-1546).
Copyright © 1987 by Michael Perry/Jubilate Hymns Ltd.;
USA © 1987 by Hope Publishing Company, Carol Stream, IL 60188.

Tune: Lindow/Norman Warren—L.M. (8.8.8.8.)

38.

From highest heaven where praises ring
(from highest heaven where praises ring)
  good news I bring (good news I bring)
  songs to sing (songs to sing):
'Jesus is born to be your king!'
('Jesus is born to be your king!')

He who in majesty arrayed
(he who in majesty arrayed)
  without our aid (without our aid),
  all has made (all has made):
see him in humble manger laid,
(see him in humble manger laid).

Let human power and pomp and pride
(let human power and pomp and pride),
both far and wide (both far and wide),
  be denied (be denied):
God is come down at Christmastide
(God is come down at Christmastide)!

To God the Father, Spirit, Son
(to God the Father, Spirit, Son),
  the Three-in-one (the Three-in-One),
  praise be done (praise be done)
for grace and hope this day begun
(for grace and hope this day begun)!

After M. Luther (1483-1546).
Copyright © 1986 by Michael Perry/Jubilate Hymns Ltd.;
USA © 1986 by Hope Publishing Company, Carol Stream, IL 60188.

Tune: Echo Carol/Martin Luther (1483-1546)—Unique

39.

From time beyond my memory
   your love has been my rock, O Lord;
since childhood days I trusted you,
   and in my youth declared your word:

But when the years are passing by,
   as friends depart and spirits fail,
O God come quickly to my side
   that in your strength I may prevail.

We praise you, God, the Holy One,
   proclaim your love from day to day;
exalt your triumphs to the skies
   and trust your mercy, come what may:

Sing glory to the Father, Son—
   and to the Spirit glory be;
let hymns to God begun on earth
   resound through all eternity!

From Psalm 71.
Copyright © 1989 by Michael Perry/Jubilate Hymns Ltd.;
USA © 1989 by Hope Publishing Company, Carol Stream, IL 60188.

Tune: Passons/Keith Landis or O Tannenbaum/German traditional—L.M. (8.8.8.8.)

40.

Gabriel the angel came
to greet the virgin Mary:
'Peace!' he said, and called her name,
'For joyful news I carry:
the Lord of all from realms above
has looked upon your soul in love;
  you shall give birth
  to Christ on earth,
  the Savior;
you bear the hope of grace—
the mark of heaven's favor,
and all shall see God's face.'

Mary asked, 'How can it be:
my love is given to no-one,
Joseph is betrothed to me—
can what is done be undone?'
'The Spirit comes—and this is how
God's power will be upon you now:
  Don't be afraid
  what God has said
  will cheer you—
the promise is not vain—
all people shall revere you,
and virtue shall remain.'

Mary then with joy replied
'I serve the Lord of heaven:
God shall be my hope and guide—
to God my heart is given
who lowly stoops to fill my cup
and raise this humble servant up.
   God's will this day
   I shall obey
   rejoicing:
then let the nations sing,
such love and mercy voicing,
and praise their Lord and king!'

From the Latin.
Copyright © 1986 by Michael Perry/Jubilate Hymns Ltd.;
USA © 1986 by Hope Publishing Company, Carol Stream, IL 60188.

Tune: Angelus ad virginem/14th Century English—Unique

41.

Give thanks to God, for he is good,
give thanks to him, the God of gods,
give thanks to him, the Lord of lords:
    his love shall last for ever!

For God alone works miracles;
the skies were made at his command,
he spread the seas upon the earth:
    his love shall last for ever!

He made the stars to shine at night,
he made the sun to shine by day;
he brought us out from slavery:
    his love shall last for ever!

He leads us onward by his grace,
he saves us from our enemies—
give thanks to God, for he is good:
    his love shall last for ever!

From Psalm 136.
Copyright © 1986 by Michael Perry/Jubilate Hymns Ltd.;
USA © 1986 by Hope Publishing Company, Carol Stream, IL 60188.

Tune: I saw three ships/English traditional melody—8.8.8.7.

42.

Given by grace,
received by faith,
  our holy food!
Token of peace,
the soul's release,
  the Bread of God:

Promise of heaven,
our sins forgiven
  through love divine!
Word of the Lord,
'This cup—my blood,'
  the saving sign.

Praise to his name
who loved and came
  our hope to be!
'This grace renew,
and when you do,
  remember me.'

Tune: none as yet—4.4.4.4.4.4.

43.

Glad music fills the Christmas sky—
a hymn of praise, a song of love;
the angels worship high above
and Mary sings her lullaby.

Of tender love for God she sings—
the chosen mother of the Son;
she knows that wonders have begun,
and trusts for all the future brings.

The angel chorus of the skies
who come to tell us of God's grace
have yet to know his human face,
to watch him die, to see him rise.

Let praise be true and love sincere,
rejoice to greet the savior's birth;
let peace and honor fill the earth
and mercy reign—for God is here!

Then lift your hearts and voices high,
sing once again the Christmas song;
for love and praise to Christ belong—
in shouts of joy, and lullaby.

Tune: Deus tuorum militum/Grenobale *Antiphoner* (1753), O Waly, Waly/English
traditional melody, Rockhaven/Roger Mayor—L.M. (8.8.8.8.)

44.

Glory and honor,
wisdom and splendor,
Lord of creation,
are yours alone:
all of earth's creatures
in exultation
sing to the Lamb upon the throne.

Once was the ransom
paid for our freedom;
from every nation
with you we reign:
yours be the praises,
high veneration,
worship for evermore. Amen.

From *Glory and honor* (Revelation 4 and 5).
Copyright © 1989 by Michael Perry/Jubilate Hymns Ltd.;
USA © 1989 by Hope Publishing Company, Carol Stream, IL 60188.

Tune: Schonster Herr Jesu/*Silesian Folk Songs* Leipzig (1842)—5.5.9.5.5.8.

45.

Glory be to God in heaven,
peace to those who love you well;
on the earth let all your people
speak your grace, your wonders tell:
Lord, we praise you for your glory,
mighty Father, heaven's king;
hear our joyful adoration
and accept the thanks we bring.

Only Son of God the Father,
Lamb who takes our sin away,
now with God in triumph seated—
for your mercy, Lord, we pray:
Jesus Christ, most high and holy,
Savior, you are God alone
in the glory of the Father
with the Spirit: Three-in-One!

From Gloria in Excelsis.
Copyright © 1982 by Michael Perry/Jubilate Hymns Ltd.;
USA © 1982 by Hope Publishing Company, Carol Stream, IL 60188.

Tune: Ode to Joy/L van Beethoven (1720-1827)—8.7.8.7.D.

46.

'Glory in the highest heaven,
  grace and peace on earth!'
To our world a Son is given,
  songs attend his birth:
come with angel hosts to name him,
  then proclaim him—tell his worth!

Shepherds, these glad tidings hearing,
  leave their flock and fold,
seek the place of Christ's appearing—
  David's town of old:
come to worship and adore him,
  kneel before him and behold!

Wise men travel with their treasure,
  frankincense they bring,
myrrh and gold in royal measure—
  this their offering;
come in homage, drawing near him
  to revere him—mighty king!

Christ is born! the sure salvation
  for a world of wrong,
light of every generation,
  hope awaited long:
come with joyful faith to meet him,
  gladly greet him with a song!

Tune: Angel voices/E G Monk (1819-1900)—8.5.8.5.8.7.

47.

Glory to the Lord of love—
in your heart proclaim his ways;
for he lifts the humble up,
for the lowly sing his praise:
　　so let us love the Lord!

Glory to the Lord of life—
he has shown his mighty deeds;
with his arm he slays the proud,
with his hand he meets our needs:
　　so let us thank the Lord!

Glory to the Lord of years—
now and evermore the same;
once he vowed to Abraham,
still his people trust his name:
　　so let us praise the Lord!

From Luke 1 (Magnificat).
Copyright © 1994 by Michael Perry/Jubilate Hymns Ltd.;
USA © 1994 by Hope Publishing Company, Carol Stream, IL 60188.

Tune: Mary's Salidumay (after a Kalinga melody) Henry W Kiley—7.7.7.7.6.

48.

God is king—be warned, you mighty;
God is judge through all the land:
order your affairs with justice,
rule with firm but gentle hand.

Help the weak, support the needy,
take to heart the fatherless;
prove the rights of those who suffer,
meet the poor in their distress.

There are lands that have no honor,
hear no wisdom, see no light;
blind, they stumble in the darkness,
leaderless they shake with fright.

Tremble, all you mighty rulers;
every nation, know God's worth:
power and wealth are God's possession—
who alone shall judge the earth!

From Psalm 82.
Copyright © 1989 by Michael Perry/Jubilate Hymns Ltd.;
USA © 1989 by Hope Publishing Company, Carol Stream, IL 60188.

Tune: Gott will's machen/J L Steiner (1668-1761)
or Llanymawddwy/David Preston—8.7.8.7.D.

49. *UK*

God is our fortress and our rock,
our mighty help in danger,
who shields us from the battle's shock
and thwarts the devil's anger:
    for still the prince of night
    prolongs his evil fight;
    he uses every skill
    to work his wicked will—
no earthly force is like him.

Our hope is fixed on Christ alone,
the Man, of God's own choosing;
without him nothing can be won
and fighting must be losing:
    so let the powers accursed
    come on and do their worst,
    the Son of God shall ride,
    to battle at our side,
and he shall have the victory.

The word of God will not be slow
while demon hordes surround us,
though evil strike its cruelest blow
and death and hell confound us:
    for even if distress
    should take all we possess,
    and those who mean us ill
    should ravage, wreck, or kill,
God's kingdom is immortal!

After Martin Luther,(1483-1546).
Copyright © 1982 by Michael Perry/Jubilate Hymns Ltd.;
USA © 1982 by Hope Publishing Company, Carol Stream, IL 60188.

Tune: Ein Feste Burg/Martin Luther (1483-1546)—8.7.8.7.6.6.6.6.7.

50. *USA*

God is our fortress and our rock,
our mighty help in danger,
who shields us from the battle's shock
and thwarts the devil's anger:
    for still the prince of night
    prolongs evil's fight;
    he uses every skill
    to work his wicked will—
no earthly force is like him.

Our hope is fixed on Christ alone,
the Man, of God's own choosing;
without him nothing can be won
and fighting must be losing:
    so let the powers accursed
    come try do their worst,
    the Son of God shall ride
    to battle at our side,
and he shall have the victory.

The word of God will not be slow
while demon hordes surround us,
though evil strike its cruelest blow
and death and hell confound us:
    for though we meet distress,
    lose all we possess,
    those planning our ill
    may ravage, wreck, or kill,
God's kingdom is immortal!

After Martin Luther,(1483-1546).
Copyright © 1982, 1987 by Michael Perry/Jubilate Hymns Ltd.;
USA © 1982, 1987 by Hope Publishing Company, Carol Stream, IL 60188.

Tune: Ein Feste Burg ('Rhythmic')/Martin Luther (1483-1546)—8.7.8.7.6.5.6.6.7.

51.

God is with the righteous—
they shall not be moved;
God is with the righteous—
they shall not be moved:
just like a tree growing by the river-side
they shall not be moved.

WOMEN They shall not—
MEN   they shall not be moved;
WOMEN they shall not—
MEN   they shall not be moved:
ALL   just like a tree growing
            by the river-side
        they shall not be moved!

God condemns the wicked—
they shall be removed;
God condemns the wicked—
they shall be removed:
just like the chaff
     blowing in the wind all day
they shall be removed.

WOMEN They shall be—
MEN   they shall be removed;
WOMEN they shall be—
MEN   they shall be removed:
ALL   just like the chaff
            blowing in the wind all day
        they shall be removed!

Happy when we hear him—
we shall not be moved;
happy when we hear him—
we shall not be moved:
just like a tree growing by the river-side
we shall not be moved.

WOMEN we shall not—

MEN   we shall not be moved;

WOMEN we shall not—

MEN   we shall not be moved:

ALL   just like a tree
                growing by the river-side
         we shall not be moved!

Happy when we love him . . .

Happy when we serve him . . .

When we read the Bible . . .

If we follow Jesus . . .

From Psalm 1.
Copyright © 1990 by Michael Perry/Jubilate Hymns Ltd.;
USA © 1990 by Hope Publishing Company, Carol Stream, IL 60188.

Tune: American traditonal melody—Unique

52.

God of light and life's creation,
reigning over all supreme,
daunting our imagination,
prospect glorious yet unseen:
 Lord, whom earth and heaven obey,
 turn towards this house today!

God of alien, God of stranger,
named by nations of the earth;
poor and exile in a manger,
God of harsh and humble birth:
 let us all with love sincere
 learn to welcome strangers here.

God of justice in our nation,
fearing neither rich nor strong,
granting truth its vindication,
passing sentence on all wrong:
 Lord, by whom we die or live,
 hear, and as you hear, forgive.

God the Father, Son and Spirit,
Trinity of love and grace,
through your mercy we inherit
word and worship in this place:
 let our children all their days
 to this house return with praise!

From I Kings 8.
Copyright © 1982 by Michael Perry/Jubilate Hymns Ltd.;
USA © 1982 by Hope Publishing Company, Carol Stream, IL 60188.

Tune: Bushey Hall/David Iliff
or All Saints/*Geistreiches Gesangbuch* (1698)—8.7.8.7.7.7.

53.

God our Father, bless your people
  that we may be one;
one in heart and one in worship,
  love's communion.

Christ our Savior, keep your people
  that we may be one;
one in prayer and one in service,
  joyful union.

Holy Spirit, guide your people
  that we may be one;
one in faith and one in purpose,
  truth's dominion.

Praise together God almighty,
  serving Christ alone;
in the Spirit be united:
  God is Three in One!

Tune: Union/David Iliff, or Sharnbrook/Paul Edwards—8.5.8.5.

54.

God save and bless our nation,
   be all our inspiration;
in every generation
   make hatred cease:
let love and justice guide us,
   nor fear nor greed divide us;
come, Lord, and walk beside us—
   grant us your peace!

Lord, be our true confession,
   our hope, our faith's possession;
so hear our intercession,
   help us to stand:
not by the strength you gave us,
   nor pride that you forgave us,
but for your glory save us—
   God bless our land!

Tune: Bramshill/Michael Perry or Roxeth/John Barnard—7.7.7.4.D.

55.

God speaks—the Lord of all the earth
and calls the world to hear:
what glory shines, what light springs forth,
to draw the people near!

Says God, the righteous one, the wise,
'Your worship I decline;
I have no need of sacrifice
for all the world is mine.

'Yet honor me, fulfill your vow,
in truth prepare the road—
so to the faithful I will show
the saving grace of God.'

Then lift your hearts and voices high
to Father, Spirit, Son;
acclaim the Three in majesty,
our God for ever One! (Amen.)

From Psalm 50.
Copyright © 1989 by Michael Perry/Jubilate Hymns Ltd.;
USA © 1989 by Hope Publishing Company, Carol Stream, IL 60188.

Tune: Christmas Eve/English traditional—D.C.M. (8.6.8.6.D.)

56.

God the Father caused to be
all we can or cannot see,
life itself, creative, free:
   we believe in God.

Christ the everlasting Word,
who for us the cross endured,
is our true and living Lord:
   we believe in God.

God the Spirit, as a dove
sent in mercy from above,
brings us life and power and love:
   we believe in God.

One-in-Three and Three-in-One!
To the Father, Spirit, Son
be all praise and honor done:
   'We believe in God!'

Tune: Capetown/F Filitz (1804-1876), Hayle/Michael Perry—7.7.7.5.

57.
God the Father of creation,
master of the realms sublime,
Lord of light and life's foundation:
  we believe and trust in him.

Christ who came from highest heaven,
God from God before all time,
Son for our redemption given:
  we believe and trust in him.

Spirit, God in us residing,
power of life and love supreme,
intercessor—pleading, guiding:
  we believe and trust in him.

Trinity of adoration!
earth responds to heaven's theme;
one the church's acclamation:
  we believe and trust in him!

Tune: Shipston/English trditional melody—8.7.8.7.

58.

God whose love we cannot measure,
  hear our song of thanks, we pray!
Who could ever count the blessings
  that surround us every day?
For you give us light in darkness,
  in our weakness make us strong;
by your peace and tender comfort
  turn our sorrow into song.

In our hearts we bless and praise you—
  you have borne our heavy load;
here we thank you for your goodness—
  we your people, you our God:
Father, Son and Holy Spirit,
  Lord whose name we lift above,
you are Love from everlasting
  and to everlasting Love.

After St. Boniface (680—754).
Copyright © 1989 by Michael Perry/Jubilate Hymns Ltd.;
USA © 1989 by Hope Publishing Company, Carol Stream, IL 60188.

Tune: Lux Eoi/A Sullivan 1842-1900; or Everton/H T Smart (1813—1879);
or Song of Thanks/Christopher Norton—8.7.8.7.D.

59.

God will arise
because the weak are crying,
God will arise
because the needy call;
God will arise
who knows and loves them all.

Flawless are God's mighty words—
silver forged in fire,
shaming every evil tongue,
every dark desire.
    God will arise . . .

When the wicked strut about,
when they take the sword,
hear your people in their pain,
come to us, O Lord!
    God will arise . . .

From Psalm 12.
Copyright © 1990 by Michael Perry/Jubilate Hymns Ltd.;
USA © 1990 by Hope Publishing Company, Carol Stream, IL 60188.

Tune: Salvum me fac/Anthony Greening—Unique

60.

Happiness is simple trust
that God is good and God is just;
the poor who have no worldly cares—
the kingdom of our God is theirs.

Happiness is sorrow's tears,
that mourn the passing of the years
till truth shall lead and justice reign,
and God shall come with joy again.

Happiness is that desire
to do what right and good require;
and all who make this rule their guide
shall find their hunger satisfied.

Happiness is humble ways,
the single mind that love displays:
all these—the lowly, pure and kind—
shall see God's face and know God's mind.

Happiness that will not cease,
is patient striving after peace;
the persecuted, God will bless—
they are the heirs of happiness!

From Matthew 5/The Beatitudes.

Tune: none as yet—7.8.8.8.

61.

Happy Christmas, everybody!
all the world is singing;
come to worship, everybody,
praise and glory bringing:
    Come to greet the Lord with joy;
    come to worship and adore him . . .

Happy Christmas everybody!
join the people praying;
God is speaking, everybody,
praise and glory bringing:
    Come to greet . . .

Happy Christmas everybody!
God's new day is dawning;
meet the savior, everybody—
Christ is born this morning:
    Come to greet . . .

Happy Christmas, everybody!
Christ is born this morning.

Tune: Jubilate, everybody (original)/Michael Perry—Unique

62.

He lives in us, the Christ of God,
  his Spirit joins with ours;
he brings to us the Father's grace
  with powers beyond our powers.
So when enticing sin grows strong,
  and human nature fails,
God's Spirit in our inner self
  fights for us, and prevails.

Our pangs of guilt and fears of death
  are Satan's stratagems—
by Jesus Christ who died for us
  God pardons: who condemns?
And when we cannot feel our faith,
  nor bring ourselves to pray,
the Spirit pleads with God for us
  in words we could not say.

God gave the Son to save us all—
  no greater love is known!
And shall that love abandon us
  who have become Christ's own?
For God has raised him from the grave,
  in this we stand assured;
so none can tear us from God's love
  in Jesus Christ our Lord.

From Romans 8.
Copyright © 1980 by Michael Perry/Jubilate Hymns Ltd.;
USA © 1980 by Hope Publishing Company, Carol Stream, IL 60188.

Tune: Rachel/Chris Bowater or Kingsfold/English traditional—C.M. (8.6.8.6.)

63.

Heal me, hands of Christ,
and search out all my pain;
restore my hope, remove my fear
and bring me peace again.

Cleanse me, blood of Christ,
take bitterness away;
let me forgive as one forgiven
and bring me peace today.

Know me, mind of Christ,
and show me all my sin;
dispel the memories of guilt,
and bring me peace within.

Fill me, joy of Christ:
anxiety shall cease
and heaven's serenity be mine,
for Christ shall bring me peace!

Tune: none as yet—5.6.8.6.

64.

Heal me, hands of Jesus,
and search out all my pain;
restore my hope, remove my fear
and bring me peace again.

Cleanse me, blood of Jesus,
take bitterness away;
let me forgive as one forgiven
and bring me peace today.

Know me, mind of Jesus,
and show me all my sin;
dispel the memories of guilt,
and bring me peace within.

Fill me, joy of Jesus:
anxiety shall cease
and heaven's serenity be mine,
for Jesus brings me peace!

Tune: Sutton Common/Norman Warren; Southwell adapted/Herbert Irons
(1861)—6.6.8.6.

65.

Hear me, O Lord, and respond to my prayer,
guard well my life, for I love you:
nothing compares with the wonders you do,
for there is no god above you.

Bring me your joy as I worship you, Lord,
come to my heart, for I need you;
teach me your way, let me walk in your truth—
I cannot fail when I heed you.

Give me a sign of your goodness, O Lord,
grant me the strength that obeys you:
you are compassion, abounding in love,
you are my king, and I praise you.

From Psalm 86.
Copyright © 1989 by Michael Perry/Jubilate Hymns Ltd.;
USA © 1989 by Hope Publishing Company, Carol Stream, IL 60188.

Tune: Pamela/Gareth Green or Thursford Green/Derek Williams—10.8.10.8.

66.

Hear the skies around
fill with joyful sound,
and the praise of angels ring;
hear the skies . . .
    Singing 'Glory in the highest,'
    singing 'Glory to the King!'
Hear the skies . . .

'To the earth be peace,
fear and sorrow cease!'
is the birthday news they bring.
'To the earth . . .
    Singing 'Glory in the highest,'
    singing 'Glory to the King!'
'To the earth . . .

Banish all dismay,
for on Christmas day
there's a song of hope to sing;
banish all . . .
    Singing 'Glory in the highest,'
    singing 'Glory to the King!'
Banish all . . .

After the Jugoslavian Carol.
Copyright © 1986 by Michael Perry/Jubilate Hymns Ltd.;
USA © 1986 by Hope Publishing Company, Carol Stream, IL 60188.

Tune: Rajske strune zadonite/Jugoslavian carol melody—Unique

67.

Here we come a-carolling
to greet our new-born king,
to join with shepherds on the hill
and hear the angels sing.
    Heaven's peace be to you,
    and to all your loved ones too;
    and God bless you
    and send you a happy new year;
    and God send you a happy new year.

Here we come a-hurrying
to see our saviour true,
to kneel and wonder at his crib
as all good Christians do.
    Heaven's peace . . .

Here we come a-worshipping
the Christ of Christmas Day,
for Mary's child, the Lord of all,
is laid upon the hay.
    Heaven's peace . . .

Here we come a-carolling
to bring your heaven's word:
so hear our song, receive our news,
and greet him as your Lord!
    Heaven's peace . . .

Tune: Wassail Song/English traditional melody—Unique

68.

How blessed are those who live by faith,
delighting in God's sure command;
for rich in grace will be their homes,
their children mighty in the land:

How happy those who freely give,
who justly deal and kindly care;
for in their darkness light shall dawn,
and long shall be their memory here:

How joyful those who, strong for truth,
rely upon the Lord most high;
unlike the wicked they shall live,
and lift their heads up to the sky!

Then praise the Lord—let joyful praise
to Father, Spirit, Son be given;
to God who loved us, came to save
and fills our hearts with grace from heaven!

From Psalm 112.
Copyright © 1989 by Michael Perry/Jubilate Hymns Ltd.;
USA © 1989 by Hope Publishing Company, Carol Stream, IL 60188.

Tune: Cross Deep/Barry Rose
or Morning Hymn/F H Barthelemon (1741-1808)—L.M. (8.8.8.8.)

69.

How shall they hear the word of God
unless the truth is told?
How shall the sinful be set free,
the sorrowful consoled?
   To all who speak the truth today
   impart your Spirit, Lord, we pray.

How shall they call to God for help
unless they have believed?
How shall the poor be given hope,
the prisoners reprieved?
   To those who help the blind to see
   give light and love and clarity.

How shall the gospel be proclaimed
that sinners may repent?
How shall the world find peace at last
if heralds are not sent?
   So send us, Lord, for we rejoice
   to speak of Christ with life and voice!

From Romans 10.
Copyright © 1981 by Michael Perry/Jubilate Hymns Ltd.;
USA © 1981 by Hope Publishing Company, Carol Stream, IL 60188.

Tune: Auch jetzt macht Gott/*Koch's Choral Buch* (1816)
or O Jesu/*Evangelisches Gesangbuch (1741)*
or Solent/Michael Perry—8.6.8.6.8.8.

70.

Hush, little baby; peace little boy
slumbering in the hay;
dream while we carol tidings of joy,
Jesus of Christmas day.

Angels will tell news of good cheer,
glory will light the sky;
shepherds will kneel wondering here,
worshipping God most high.
Hush, little baby . . .

Joseph will guard, Mary will smile,
holding in sweet embrace
heaven's true Lord, here for a while,
Jesus, God's gift of grace.
Hush, little baby . . .

Wise men from far, soon they will come,
worship and gifts they bring;
incense for prayer, myrrh for a tomb,
gold to reveal a king.
Hush, little baby . . .

Tune: Skye Boat Song/Scottish traditional melody—Unique

71.

I believe in God the Father
who created heaven and earth,
holding all things in his power,
bringing light and life to birth.

I believe in God the Savior,
Son of Man and Lord most high,
crucified to be redeemer,
raised to life that death may die.

I believe in God the Spirit,
wind of heaven and flame of fire,
pledge of all that we inherit,
sent to comfort and inspire.

Honor, glory, might and merit
be to God, and God alone!
Father, Son and Holy Spirit,
One-in-Three and Three-in-One.

Tune: All for Jesus/J Stainer (1840-1901)—8.7.8.7.

72.

I cried out for heaven to hear me,
I reached out to God for my help;
no counsel or comfort would cheer me,
my spirit abandoned all hope.

But in my despair I remembered
the songs of a long time ago,
and dreamed of the majesty splendored
of God the almighty, the true:

You spoke in the wind and the thunder,
the earth and the elements shook;
your power tore the waters asunder,
as Shepherd, you guided your flock.

Then thank you, O God for your merit,
your faithfulness always the same;
the Father, the Son and the Spirit—
one Lord over all: praise your name!

From Psalm 77.
Copyright © 1989 by Michael Perry/Jubilate Hymns Ltd.;
USA © 1989 by Hope Publishing Company, Carol Stream, IL 60188.

Tune: Now join we/Michael Metcalf—9.8.9.8.

73.

 I love you, Lord, my Rock and my Redeemer;
 you make me strong, I trust in you always.
 You are my shield, the hope of my salvation;
 I cry to you, and offer you my praise.

The seas of death—their torrents overwhelm me;
in my perplexity I call upon the Lord;
and from your heaven you hear my voice and answer me,
and, reaching down, you save me by your word.
 I love you, Lord . . .

The mountains shake—they tremble at your anger,
like burning coals your fire consumes the skies;
you tear the clouds, the lightning strikes your enemies,
you guides me in your ways and makes me wise.
 I love you, Lord . . .

My Savior lives—his mercy has delivered me,
he raised me up to this exalted place;
I worship him who lets me share his victories
and evermore will follow me with grace.
 I love you, O Lord . . .

From Psalm 18.
Copyright © 1990 by Michael Perry/Jubilate Hymns Ltd.;
USA © 1990 by Hope Publishing Company, Carol Stream, IL 60188.

Tune: by Christopher Norton—Irregular

74.

I praise you, Lord, with all my heart,
rejoicing in your wonders!

Your justice is perfect,
your judgments are true,
the wicked have fallen,
their names are forgotten:
I praise you, Lord . . .

You govern the peoples,
you help the oppressed,
and no-one who seeks you,
is ever forsaken:
I praise you, Lord . . .

From Psalm 9.
Copyright © 1990 by Michael Perry/Jubilate Hymns Ltd.;
USA © 1990 by Hope Publishing Company, Carol Stream, IL 60188.

Tune: Confitebor tibi/David Llewellyn Green—Unique

75.

I will give thanks to the Lord most high;
I will sing praise to his righteous name.

I have no strength but yours,
O God, my hiding-place;
you snatch me from the lion's claws
and save me by your grace.
    I will give thanks . . .

To love that will not cease
I owe my life, my all;
and justly if I break God's peace
then punishment will fall.
    I will give thanks . . .

My God, my sovereign still,
my shield, my joy, my crown:
you honor those who do your will,
you tread the evil down.
    I will give thanks . . .

From Psalm 7.
Copyright © 1990 by Michael Perry/Jubilate Hymns Ltd.;
USA © 1990 by Hope Publishing Company, Carol Stream, IL 60188.

Tune: Hiding-place/David Iliff, I have no strength but yours/Chris Rolinson—Unique

76.

If we love the word of God
  and heed it day and night;
if we make God's truth our law,
  God's counsel our delight . . .

If we shun the sinners' way
  and spurn their false advice;
if we turn from Godless lies
  and evils that entice . . .

If we do these things we'll find
  rich blessings as we go;
then we'll flourish like a tree
  where living waters flow.

From Psalm 1.
Copyright © 1989 by Michael Perry/Jubilate Hymns Ltd.;
USA © 1989 by Hope Publishing Company, Carol Stream, IL 60188.

Tune: Fullness/Noel Tredinnick or Dartmeet/David Peacock—7.6.7.6.

77.

I'll praise you, Lord, with heart content and joyful,
before the world I'll tell your righteous ways;
I will bow down towards your holy temple,
exalt your name and sing your worthy praise.

Beyond the skies you set your timeless kingdom—
your word shall last, your throne shall never fall;
the lords of earth will marvel at your wisdom
and kneel before the mighty Lord of all.

Though set on high, you look upon the lowly—
the proud you see with sorrow from afar;
in all my trouble you are swift to save me,
and with your arm restrain the threat of war.

For ever you will keep your face towards us,
your mercy and your love will never cease:
then come, fulfill in us your mighty purpose,
and grant to your creation perfect peace.

From Psalm 138.
Copyright © 1989 by Michael Perry/Jubilate Hymns Ltd.;
USA © 1989 by Hope Publishing Company, Carol Stream, IL 60188.

Tune: Highwood/R R Terry (1865-1938) or O perfect love/J Barnby (1838-1896)—11.10.11.10.

78.
In a stable, in a manger,
lies a baby—our true savior:
hear the carol that we sing you,
and the tidings that we bring you.
  There's a light in the heavens this morning
  and a song for the angels to sing;
  in a stable, in a manger,
  lies a baby—our true savior.

There the virgin mother Mary
tends her infant—oh so gently;
and the beauty of the God-head
shines around him—her belovèd.
  There's a light in the heavens . . .

Let the mighty faint and tremble
at the triumph of the humble;
and the guilty leave their sighing
where the sinner's hope is lying.
  There's a light in the heavens . . .

Tune: Esta noche/Spanish carol melody—Unique

79. *UK*

In Christ there is no east or west,
in him no pride of birth;
the chosen family God has blessed
now spans the whole wide earth.

For God in Christ has made us one
from every land and race;
has reconciled us through the Son,
and met us all with grace.

It is by grace we are assured
that we belong to him:
the love we share in Christ our Lord,
the Spirit's work within.

So brothers, sisters, praise his name
who died to set us free
from sin, division, hate and shame,
from spite and enmity!

In Christ there is no east or west—
he breaks all barriers down:
by Christ redeemed, by Christ possessed,
in Christ we live as one.

From a first line by W A Dunkerley (1852-1941).
(See alternative version below)
Copyright © 1982 by Michael Perry/Jubilate Hymns Ltd.;
USA © 1982 by Hope Publishing Company, Carol Stream, IL 60188.

Tune: McKee/American traditional
or St. Bernard/*Tochter Zion* Cologne 1741, St. Stephen (CM)/W Jones (1726-
1800)—C.M. (8.6.8.6.)

80. *USA*

In Christ there is no East or West,
in Christ no South or North;
but only those by God possessed
throughout the whole wide earth.

For God in Christ has made us one
from every land and race,
has reconciled us through the Son
and made us whole by grace.

So brothers, sisters, praise his name
who died to set us free
from sin, division, hate and shame,
from spite and enmity!

In Christ now meet both East and West,
in Christ meet South and North—
one joyful people God has blessed
throughout the whole wide earth.

From a first line by W A Dunkerley (1852-1941)
(See alternative version above).
Copyright © 1982, 1989 by Michael Perry/Jubilate Hymns Ltd.;
USA © 1982, 1989 by Hope Publishing Company, Carol Stream, IL 60188.

Tune: McKee/American traditional or St. Bernard/*Tochter Zion* Cologne 1741, St.
Stephen (CM)/W Jones (1726-1800)—C.M. (8.6.8.6.)

81.

In majesty and splendor
and robes of light endowed
is God who spreads the heavens
and rides upon the cloud,
with flame and fire as servants,
as messenger, the wind—
O honour God with worship,
give praise, all humankind!

The earth you set securely
and covered with a cloak
of waters over mountains
which, at your bidding, broke;
and, from the voice of thunder
down rivers fled the rain
to where, by your provision,
the waters shall remain.

To us you give the harvest,
give animals to feed;
to every suppliant creature
the graces that we need.
The woodland tree is watered,
where birds may build their nest,
while high upon the mountains
wild creatures find their rest.

You spread the shades of darkness,
you forge the day-time heat,
you teach the moon the seasons,
the sun to rise and set.
For beasts you make the night-time
till dawn to hunt their prey;
for us, the light till evening
to labour through the day.

The bounds of your creation—
they cannot be apprised,
and countless are the wonders
your wisdom has devised.
Yet what are we without you?
You hide your face—we die:
so while life lasts, we worship
and praise you, God most high.

From Psalm 104.
Copyright © 1973 by Michael Perry/Jubilate Hymns Ltd.;
USA © 1983 by Hope Publishing Company, Carol Stream, IL 60188.

Tune: Majesty and Splendor/Norman Warren—7.6.7.6.D.

82.

In the darkness of the night
the people walk in sorrow;
they have not seen, nor can they know
the light that dawns tomorrow.
　　For a Child is born to us;
　　to us a Son is given:
　　his holy name—the Prince of peace,
　　the Mighty God of heaven.

In the darkness of the night
a host of angels gather
to greet the Wonderful, the Wise,
the Everlasting Father.
　　For a Child . . .

In the darkness of the night
where Judah's hills lie dreaming,
the virgin mother of the Christ
beholds our world's redeeming.
　　For a Child . . .

From Isaiah 9.
Copyright © 1987 by Michael Perry/Jubilate Hymns Ltd.;
USA © 1987 by Hope Publishing Company, Carol Stream, IL 60188.

Tune: Yr hen gelynnen/Welsh traditional melody—7.7.8.7.D.

83.

In the streets of every city,
bringing hope and healing strife,
living out the Savior's pity,
caring for each precious life:
　　where it matters, there you'll find us
　　in the service of our Lord.

Through the world, in every nation,
serving Christ with lives made whole;
in his name we speak salvation—
grace for every seeking soul:
　　where it matters, there you'll find us
　　thrilling those who have not heard.

In our daily time of praying,
thanking God for sins forgiven,
hearing what his voice is saying,
tasting now the joys of heaven:
　　where it matters there you'll find us,
　　silent, waiting on his word.

At his table, there you'll find us
pouring wine and sharing bread;
'Christ has died' these gifts remind us,
'Christ is risen from the dead':
　　where it matters, there you'll find us,
　　hearts renewed and lives restored.

God of city, state and nation,
Lord ascended, coming King:
with resounding exultation
of your faithfulness we sing:
　　when it matters, then you'll find us
　　and for ever be adored.

Tune: by Chris Rolinson—8.7.8.7.8.7.

Jesus, child of Mary

Gently
Descant

4 An - gel hosts the skies a - dorn,

1 Je - sus, child of Ma - ry born,
2 To this place of pain and fear
3 In - fant in a man - ger laid,
4 An - gel hosts the skies a - dorn,

we with shep-herds glo - ri - fy Je - sus, child of

Son of God and Lord most high; come to wear a
love de - scends in hu - man guise; God in Christ self -
wrapped a - bout with pea - sant shawl; gift of grace so
we with shep-herds glo - ri - fy Je - sus, child of

Ma - ry born, Son of God most high.

crown of thorn, brave - ly come to die.
- emp - tied here, fool - ish - ness most wise:
free - ly made, sav - ior for us all.
Ma - ry born, Son of God most high.

Alternative tune: Charity

Words: Michael Perry
Music: Michael Perry, arranged with descant by Norman Warren

Hayle
7775

84.

Jesus, child of Mary born,
Son of God and Lord most high;
come to wear a crown of thorn,
  bravely come to die.

To this place of pain and fear
love descends in human guise;
God in Christ self-emptied here,
  foolishness most wise:

Infant in a manger laid,
wrapped about with peasant shawl;
gift of grace so freely made,
  savior for us all.

Angel hosts the skies adorn,
we with shepherds glorify
Jesus, child of Mary born,
  Son of God most high.

Tune: Hayle/Michael Perry—7.7.7.5.

85.

Jesus Christ the Lord is born—
all the bells are ringing!
Angels greet the holy One
   and shepherds hear them singing,
   and shepherds hear them singing:

'Go to Bethlehem today,
find your king and savior:
glory be to God on high,
   to earth his peace and favor,
   to earth his peace and favor!'

WOMEN

Held within a cattle stall,
loved by love maternal,
see the master of us all,
   our Lord of lords eternal,
   our Lord of lords eternal!

MEN

Soon shall come the wise men three,
rousing Herod's anger;
mothers' hearts shall broken be
   and Mary's son in danger,
   and Mary's son in danger.

Death from life and life from death—
our salvation's story:
let all living things give breath
   to Christmas songs of glory,
   to Christmas songs of glory!

From the Latin and after German authors.
Copyright © 1982 by Michael Perry/Jubilate Hymns Ltd.;
USA © 1982 by Hope Publishing Company, Carol Stream, IL 60188.

Tune: Puer Nobis/*Piae Cantiones* (1582)/Descant: Iliff—7.6.7.7.

86.

Jesus, hope of every nation,
light of heaven upon our way;
promise of the world's salvation,
spring of life's eternal day!

Saints by faith on God depending
wait to see Messiah born;
sin's oppressive night is ending
in the glory of the dawn.

Look, he comes!—the long-awaited
Christ, redeemer, living Word;
hope and faith are vindicated
as with joy we greet the Lord.

Glory in the highest heaven
to the Father, Spirit, Son;
on the earth all praise be given
to our God, the Three-in-One!

From Luke 2—The Song of Simeon/Nunc Dimittis.
Copyright © 1973 by Michael Perry/Jubilate Hymns Ltd.;
USA © 1973 by Hope Publishing Company, Carol Stream, IL 60188.

Tune: Halton Holgate (Sharon)/later from of melody by W Boyce (1711-
1779)—8.7.8.7.

87.

Jesus is our refuge,
    he is with us always,
coming to our rescue,
    and so we will not fear.
Though the mountains tremble,
    and though the earth is shaking,
our saviour will redeem us,
    our Lord is coming near.

See the mighty river
    flowing from God's city,
blessings from the glory,
    the place where Jesus reigns
Nations are in uproar,
    the people faint from terror,
but Jesus Christ is coming
    and he will break our chains!

Come and see the wonders
    he will do from heaven,
ending all aggression
    and bringing peace to birth.
Everyone will see him
    and bow before their master;
for he will be exalted
    and praised through all the earth.

From Psalm 46 and Revelation 1.
Copyright © 1984 by Michael Perry/Jubilate Hymns Ltd.;
USA © 1983 by Hope Publishing Company, Carol Stream, IL 60188.

Tune: Dies es nuestro (Chile)—6.6.6.6.6.7.7.6.

88.
Jesus, Redeemer,
come to make my heart your home,
tenderly and quickly come;
fill me with your light,
reveal your face.

No virtue can I offer—
yet I know you love me:
once you came to die
and rose to save me by your grace.

Jesus, Redeemer,
Jesus, Redeemer, Redeemer,
forgive the hands that welcome you,
cleanse the lips that sing to you;
take my life to live for you today,
and evermore possess me in your perfect peace!

Tune: Ave Maria/J S Bach (1685-1750), adapted C F Gounod (1818-1893)—Unique

89.
Jesus, Redeemer, Mary's child,
endue me with your humble spirit!
I live, by mercy reconciled,
and all your work of grace inherit.

You come to me from heights of glory,
for me you tread this earthly road;
you know and share my human story,
and show me how to love like God.
Jesus, Redeemer!

Jesus, Redeemer, closest friend,
surround me with your tender loving!
From my beginning to my end
you lead me on,
your mercy proving.

Beneath your Cross I stand forgiven,
where from my sins I find release
and gain the first sure step to heaven
and taste the promise of your peace:
Jesus, Redeemer!

Jesus, Redeemer, holy Lord,
enthrall me with your perfect beauty!
I see your face, I hear your word,
your will becomes my joyful duty.

You brave the hurt this world devises
to die for one unkind, untrue;
yet from your tomb the new day rises—
and I shall rise to reign with you:
Jesus, Redeemer!

Tune: Ave Maria/F Schubert (1797-1828)—Unique

90.
Jesus, Savior, holy Child,
    sleep tonight,
slumber deep till morning light.
    Lullaby, our joy, our treasure,
    all our hope and all our pleasure:
at the cradle where you lie
we will worship—lullaby!

From your Father's home you come
    to this earth,
by your lowly manger birth:
    Child of God, our nature sharing;
    Son of Man, our sorrows bearing;
rich, yet here among the poor:
Christ the Lord, whom we adore!

Now to heaven's glory song
    we reply
with a Christmas lullaby.
    Hush, the eternal Lord is sleeping
    close in Mary's tender keeping:
babe on whom the angels smiled—
Jesus, Savior, holy Child.

Tune: Rocking/ Moravian or Czech traditional—7.3.7.8.8.7.7.

91.

Journey to Bethlehem, worship your king,
   worship your king, worship your king;
come with your praises and joyfully sing,
   joyfully sing, joyfully sing!

Come with your presents of honor and love,
   honor and love, honor and love;
this is the birthday of hope from above,
   hope from above, hope from above.

Come with your sorrow
     for wrongs you have done,
   wrongs you have done,
     wrongs you have done;
find your forgiveness in God's only Son,
   God's only Son, God's only Son.

Come with your praises and joyfully sing,
   joyfully sing, joyfully sing;
journey to Bethlehem, worship your king,
   worship your king, worship your king!

Copyright © 1987 by Michael Perry/Jubilate Hymns Ltd.;
USA © 1987 by Hope Publishing Company, Carol Stream, IL 60188.

Tune: Stony Brook/Norman Warren—10.8.10.8.

92.

Let the desert sing
    and the wasteland flower,
for the glory of Christ
    in its light and power
shall be seen on the hills
    where he comes to save!

Then the blind shall see
    and the deaf shall hear
and the lame shall leap
    like the fallow deer
and the voice of the silent
    shout aloud.

When the ransomed walk
    with their Lord that day
on the perfect road
    called the Sacred Way,
every tear shall give place
    to a song of joy!

From Isaiah 35.
Copyright © 1982 by Michael Perry/Jubilate Hymns Ltd.;
USA © 1982 by Hope Publishing Company, Carol Stream, IL 60188.

Tune: Elmsdale/David Iliff—10.11.11.

93.
Lift up your hearts to the Lord,
break into songs of joy;
let the sea roar, let the hills ring,
shout his glorious name!
    Harps and horns and trumpets, sound;
    praise him, all the world around!
    O sing a new song;
    O sing a new song!

Bow down and worship the Lord,
greet him who comes to reign;
share his triumph, hear his judgment,
see his marvelous works:
    Harps and horns . . .

Tell out the word of the Lord,
speak of his saving power:
sure his mercy, true his promise,
great his wonderful love!
    Harps and horns . . .

From Psalm 98 (Cantate Domino).
Copyright © 1973 by Michael Perry/Jubilate Hymns Ltd.;
USA © 1973 by Hope Publishing Company, Carol Stream, IL 60188.

Tune: Sound loud the trumpet (*Psalm Praise*)/Michael Perry, Lift your heart/Christopher
Norton—7.6.8.6.Ref.

94.

Lift your heart and raise your voice,
faithful people, come, rejoice:
grace and power are shown on earth
in the savior's holy birth.
    Gloria!

Mortals, hear what angels say;
shepherds, quickly make your way,
finding truth in lowly guise,
wisdom to confound the wise.
    Gloria!

Here he lies, the Lord of all;
nature's king in cattle-stall,
God of heaven to earth come down—
cross for throne and thorn for crown.
    Gloria!

Lift your hearts and voices high:
then shall glory fill the sky—
Christ shall come and not be long,
earth shall sing the angels' song:
    'Gloria!'

Tune: Marston St. Lawrence/Paul Edwards—7.7.7.7.3.

95.

Like a mighty river flowing,
like a flower in beauty growing,
far beyond all human knowing
   is the perfect peace of God.

Like the hills serene and even,
like the coursing clouds of heaven,
like the heart that's been forgiven
   is the perfect peace of God.

Like the summer breezes playing,
like the tall trees softly swaying,
like the lips of silent praying
   is the perfect peace of God.

Like the morning sun ascended,
like the scents of evening blended,
like a friendship never ended
   is the perfect peace of God.

Like the azure ocean swelling,
like the jewel all-excelling,
far beyond our human telling
   is the perfect peace of God.

Tunes: Old Yeavering/Noël Tredinnick, Quem pastores laudavere/14th Century German carol melody—8.8.8.7.

96.

Lord Jesus Christ, invited guest and savior,
with tender mercy hear us as we pray;
grant our desire for those who seek your favor,
come with your love and bless them both today:

Give them your strength for caring and for serving,
give them your graces—faithfulness and prayer;
make their resolve to follow you unswerving,
make their reward your peace beyond compare:

Be their delight in joy, their hope in sorrow,
be their true friend in pleasure as in pain;
guest of today and guardian of tomorrow,
turn humble water into wine again!

Tune: O perfect Love/J Barnby (1838-1896)—11.10.11.10.

97.

Lord Jesus, for my sake you come,
the Son of Man, and God most high;
you leave behind your Father's home
to live and serve, to love and die.

Your eyes seek out our world's distress
through insult, grief and agony;
they meet our tears with tenderness,
yet blaze upon our blasphemy.

Are these the robes that make men proud,
is this the crown that you must wear?
Your face is set, your head is bowed,
and silently you persevere.

You never grasped at selfish gain,
and yet your hands are marked with blood;
transfixed by nails, they cling in pain
to sorrow on a cross of wood.

Lord Jesus, come to me anew;
your hands, your eyes, your thoughts be mine.
until I learn to love like you
and live on earth the life divine.

Tune: Daniel/Irish traditional, or St. Laurence/L G Hayne (1836-1883), or
Herongate/English traditional—L.M. (8.8.8.8.)

98.

Lord Jesus, let these eyes of mine
reflect your beauty and your grace;
so joyful and so tender shine
that other eyes shall seek your face.

Lord, use my ears, for I rejoice
to hear the word of life—with awe
I listen for the whispering voice
that calls beyond the thunder's roar.

And holy Jesus, set my mind
to search for truth and know your way;
to think upon the good I find,
to spurn the night and love the day:

And may my hands, which learned their skill
at your direction, by your love,
now deftly moving at your will
console, encourage and improve.

So to your throne, O Christ, again
my sense of sight and sound I bring;
and in my mind I let you reign,
and with my hands serve you, my king:

Speak through this voice that you have given,
your love and mercy to proclaim,
until I join the choirs of heaven
and sing the glory of your name!

Tune: Herongate/English melody—L.M. (8.8.8.8.)

99.

Lord of love, you come to bless
all who will by faith confess
Jesus, God's own righteousness
   to the world made known.

Bruised on Calvary's weary road,
bowed beneath the curse of God,
shedding the atoning blood
   sacrifice is done.

By the arms you open wide,
by your wounded hands and side,
Jesus, we are justified,
   saved by grace alone!

From Romans 3.21-26
Copyright © 1987 by Michael Perry/Jubilate Hymns Ltd.;
USA © 1987 by Hope Publishing Company, Carol Stream, IL 60188.

Tune: Tama Ngakau Marie; Maori traditional melody, New Zealand—7.7.7.5.

100.

Lord, you are Love!
Love set me free;
Love for the loveless,
Love came for me.

Love, touch my heart,
Love, lift my soul;
Love, make me loving,
Love, make me whole.

Love, be my word,
Love, fill my mind;
Love, make me holy,
Love, make me kind:

Love all my days,
Love at my end;
Love for my Saviour,
Love for my Friend!

Based on 1 John 4.16
Copyright © 1991 by Michael Perry/Jubilate Hymns Ltd.;
USA © 1991 by Hope Publishing Company, Carol Stream, IL 60188.

Tune: by Norman Warren—4.4.5.4.

101.
Lullaby, little Jesus;
there you lie, little Jesus—
  as the winds bite
  on this cold night—
in the hay, little Jesus.
  As the winds bite
  on this cold night:
Lullaby, little Jesus!

Lullaby, little Jesus;
don't you cry, little Jesus:
  come tomorrow
  there'll be sorrow
and dismay, little Jesus.
  Come tomorrow,
  there'll be sorrow.
Lullaby, little Jesus!

Lullaby, little Jesus:
in the sky, little Jesus,
  there is singing,
  glory bringing
to this day, little Jesus.
  There is singing,
  glory bringing,
Lullaby, little Jesus!

After the Polish carol
Copyright © 1987 by Michael Perry/Jubilate Hymns Ltd.;
USA © 1987 by Hope Publishing Company, Carol Stream, IL 60188.

Tune: Jezus malusienki/Polish melody—Unique

102.

Mary and Joseph—praise with them:
 Jesus is born, Jesus is born;
worship this day in Bethlehem,
 Jesus is born, Jesus is born!

Angels have spoken—hear God's word,
 'Peace on the earth, peace on the earth;
he who is born is Christ the Lord,
 peace on the earth, peace on the earth!'

Shepherds have worshipped—join their song,
 'Glory to God, glory to God;
this is the savior promised long,
 glory to God, glory to God!'

See the Creator—here he lies,
 God has come down, God has come down;
love has appeared before our eyes,
 God has come down, God has come down!

Tune: Manger Dance/Norman Warren—L.M. (8.8.8.8.)

103.

Mary sang a song, a song of love,
magnified the mighty Lord above;
melodies of praise his name extol
from the very depths of Mary's soul:

'God the Lord has done great things for me,
looked upon my life's humility;
happy they shall call me from this day—
merciful is he whom we obey.

'To the humble soul our God is kind,
to the proud he brings unease of mind:
who uplifts the poor, pulls down the strong?
God alone has the power to right the wrong!

'He who has been Israel's strength and stay
fills the hungry, sends the rich away;
he has shown his promise firm and sure,
faithful to his people evermore.'

This was Mary's song as we recall,
mother to the savior of us all:
magnify his name and sing his praise,
worship and adore him, all your days!

From Luke 1 Song of Mary (Magnificat).
Copyright © 1973 by Michael Perry/Jubilate Hymns Ltd.;
USA © 1973 by Hope Publishing Company, Carol Stream, IL 60188.

Tune: Mary's Song/Michael Perry, Pavenham/Peter Brown (also adapted Perry &
Walshaw 1994), Mary sang a song (Christopher Norton)—9.9.9.9.

104.

May the Lord God hear you pray,
may God's strength be yours today;
may God bless you from above,
lifting up your heart in love.

May God give you all you need,
may God make your plans succeed;
may God guide you all your days,
filling all our hearts with praise:

Now we see the Lord can save,
now the trembling heart is brave;
now we know that Love will hear:
worship now, for God is near!

From Psalm 20.
Copyright © 1990 by Michael Perry/Jubilate Hymns Ltd.;
USA © 1990 by Hope Publishing Company, Carol Stream, IL 60188.

Tune: Queen's Terrace/Norman Warren—7.7.7.7.

105.

My faithful shepherd is the Lord,
who leads me by the pastures green
to pools of water sweet and clean,
and makes me stronger through the word.

God's promise is my certain guide,
whose way is truth, whose path is right:
'I shall not fear the darkest night
for you, O Lord, are at my side!'

'You bring to those who hate me, shame;
you spread a feast and fill my cup.
It overflows! You raise me up
to live with you and bless your name.'

To God the Father, Spirit, Son,
be glory now, until the song
of mercy through the ages long
in heaven shall greet the Three-in-One!

From Psalm 23.
Copyright © 1986 by Michael Perry/Jubilate Hymns Ltd.;
USA © 1986 by Hope Publishing Company, Carol Stream, IL 60188.

Tune: Herrongate/English melody—L.M. (8.8.8.8.)

106.

No sorrow, no mourning, no crying,
no hatred, no hurt and no lying:
but freedom and love and salvation,
and peace for each tribe and each nation:
    Raise up your kingdom, O Lord,
    bring joy to the end of our story;
    then Jesus, true to your word—
    come, reign in your power and your glory;
    then Jesus, true to your word—
    come, reign in your power and your glory!
    Alleluia, alleluia, amen!

How bright is the light of God's city,
how true is his mercy and pity!
The darkness will conquer it never,
for God is our glory for ever.
    Raise up your kingdom . . .

Such rivers in heaven are flowing,
such trees by the waters are growing!
The leaves of the trees are for healing,
God's love for the nations revealing.
    Raise up your kingdom . . .

What wonder and beauty descending,
what songs and what laughter are blending!
God's people, whose sins are forgiven—
the Bride of the Lamb—come from heaven
    Raise up your kingdom . . .

All just is our God, and all-knowing—
all-wise to our reaping and sowing:
the judge of our love or defying,
the giver of living or dying!
    Raise up your kingdom . . .

So deep is our thirst and our yearning,
so great is the hope in us burning:
we sing to our heavenly Father,
'Send Jesus. Lord, come—maranatha!'
   Raise up your kingdom . . .

From Revelation 20-22.

Tune: Um pouco além do presente—9.9.9.9.Ref.

107.

Not the grandeur of the mountains,
nor the splendor of the sea,
can excel the ceaseless wonder
of my Savior's love to me:
    for his love to me is faithful,
    and his mercy is divine;
    and his truth is everlasting,
    and his perfect peace is mine.

Not the streams that fill the valleys,
nor the clouds that drift along,
can delight me more than Jesus
or replace my grateful song:
    for his love . . .

Yet these all convey his beauty
and proclaim his power and grace—
for they are among the tokens
of the love upon his face:
    for his love . . .

Tune: Everton/H T Smart (1813-1879)—8.7.8.7.D.

108.

Now evening comes to close the day,
and soon the silent hours
shall banish all our fears away,
and sleep renew our powers.

Into your hands, eternal Friend,
we give ourselves again,
and to your watchful care commend
all those in grief or pain.

In waking, lift our thoughts above,
in sleeping guard us still,
that we may rise to know your love
and prove your perfect will.

To Father, Son and Spirit—praise,
all mortal praise be given,
till sleep at last shall end our days
and we shall wake in heaven!

After Te Lucis ante terminum (Before the ending of the day).
Copyright © 1986 by Michael Perry/Jubilate Hymns Ltd.;
USA © 1986 by Hope Publishing Company, Carol Stream, IL 60188.

Tune: Charnwood/Peter White or Stracathro/C Hutcheson (1792-1860)—C.M.
(8.6.8.6.)

109.
Now through the grace of God we claim
this life to be God's own,
baptized with water in the name
of Father, Spirit, Son.

For Jesus Christ the crucified,
who broke the power of sin,
now lives to plead for those baptized
in unity with him.

So let us act upon his word,
rejoicing in our faith,
until we rise with Christ our Lord
and triumph over death!

Tune: St. Botolph/G A Slater (1896-1979)—C.M. (8.6.8.6.)

110.

O bless the God of Israel
    who comes to set us free;
who visits and redeems us,
    and grants us liberty.
The prophets spoke of mercy,
    of rescue and release:
God shall fulfill the promise
    to bring our people peace.

He comes! the Son of David,
    the one whom God has given;
he comes to live among us
    and raise us up to heaven:
before him goes the herald,
    forerunner in the way,
the prophet of salvation,
    the messenger of Day.

Where once were fear and darkness
    the sun begins to rise—
the dawning of forgiveness
    upon the sinner's eyes,
to guide the feet of pilgrims
    along the paths of peace:
O bless our God and Savior,
    with songs that never cease!

From Luke 1/Benedictus.
(See also 'Blest be the God of Israel')
Copyright © 1973 by Michael Perry/Jubilate Hymns Ltd.;
USA © 1973 by Hope Publishing Company, Carol Stream, IL 60188.

Tune: Merle's tune, or Morning Light/G J Webb (1803-1887) or Roewen/Roger Mayor
or Thornbury/B Harwood (1859-1949)—7.6.7.6.D.

111.
'O bless the Lord, my soul!' I sing,
  and worship day and night
my God arrayed in majesty
  and robed in glorious light:

For like a tent you spread the sky,
  on chariot-clouds you ride;
and by the wind, your messenger,
  your truth is prophesied.

MEN

  You bind the sea, or loose the storm
    in lightning's primal flame;
  the rising spring and flowing stream
    cry glory to your name.

ALL

  O mighty Lord of every land,
    you know our human need,
  and all the creatures of the earth
    you guide and tend and feed.

WOMEN

  The sun and moon appear and set
    controlled by hidden force;
  the stars declare your faithfulness,
    consistent in their course.

ALL

  Yet what you give, O sovereign Lord,
    your power can take away;
  our very lives belong to you
    until our dying day.

So let me sing your worthy praise,
  your matchless grace extol
till all creation join the hymn:
  'O bless the Lord, my soul!'

From Psalm 104.
Copyright © 1990 by Michael Perry/Jubilate Hymns Ltd.;
USA © 1990 by Hope Publishing Company, Carol Stream, IL 60188.

Tune: Brightwell Baldwin/John Barnard—C.M. (8.6.8.6.)

112.

O Christ of all the ages, come!
We fear to journey on our own;
without you near we cannot face
the future months, the years unknown.

Afflicted, tempted, tried like us,
you match our moments of despair;
with us you watch the desert hours,
and in our sorrows you are there.

O Savior, fastened to a cross
by tearing nails—our selfish ways;
the grieving, caring Lord of love,
you bear the sins of all our days.

Triumphant from the grave you rise—
the morning breaks upon our sight;
and with its dawning, future years
will shine with your unending light.

O Christ of all the ages, come!
The days and months and years go by:
accept our praise, redeem our lives—
our strength for all eternity! (Amen.)

Tune: Gonfalon Royal/P C Buck (1871-1947)—L.M. (8.8.8.8.)

113.

O come, Christians, wonder
be thankful, and ponder
the birth of our savior and Lord:
for we who were sighing,
and sinning, and dying,
in Jesus are fully restored.

So lift high your voices,
as heaven rejoices
to tell of the babe in the hay:
this Jesus—the holy,
the poor, and the lowly—
we praise him and serve him today!

Let sister and brother
speak peace to each other,
and brother and sister agree:
for love is our story—
to Jesus the glory
both now and for ever shall be.

From the Welsh.
Copyright © 1987 by Michael Perry/Jubilate Hymns Ltd.;
USA © 1987 by Hope Publishing Company, Carol Stream, IL 60188.

Tune: Sarach/ Norman Warren—6.6.8.D.

114.

O come, our world's Redeemer, come!
We hail the ageless mystery
that God should grace the Virgin's womb
and take our frail humanity.

For not by mortal will or power,
but by the Holy Spirit's breath,
the seed of heaven comes to flower,
the Word made flesh is found on earth.

He comes, for whom creation yearns,
to face the realms of death alone;
and to his glory he returns
to gain a kingdom and a throne.

He comes to triumph over wrong
and bring us captive back to heaven;
for in our weakness he is strong,
and for his sake we are forgiven.

O come, our world's Redeemer, come!
Your manger shines upon our night—
so let the voice of doubt be dumb,
for none shall quench this glorious light!

From Veni Redemptor gentium.
Copyright © 1986 by Michael Perry/Jubilate Hymns Ltd.;
USA © 1986 by Hope Publishing Company, Carol Stream, IL 60188.

Tune: Splendor/M Praetorius (1571-1621)—L.M. (8.8.8.8.)

115.

O God beyond all praising,
    we worship you today
and sing the love amazing
    that songs cannot repay;
for we can only wonder
    at every gift you send,
at blessings without number
    and mercies without end:
we lift our hearts before you
    and wait upon your word,
we honor and adore you,
    our great and mighty Lord.

[The flower of earthly splendor
    in time must surely die,
its fragile bloom surrender
    to you the Lord most high;
but hidden from all nature
    the eternal seed is sown—
though small in mortal stature,
    to heaven's garden grown:
for Christ the Man from heaven
    from death has set us free,
and we through him are given
    the final victory!]

Then hear, O gracious Savior,
  accept the love we bring,
that we who know your favor
  may serve you as our king;
and whether our tomorrows
  be filled with good or ill,
we'll triumph through our sorrows
  and rise to bless you still:
to marvel at your beauty
  and glory in your ways,
and make a joyful duty
  our sacrifice of praise.

The second verse (from 1 Corinthians 15) is seasonal, and may be omitted.

Tune: Thaxted/G T Holst (1874—1934)—13.13.13.13.13.13.

116.

O God, we thank you that your name
is known and feared through all the earth;
your sentence waits the appointed time
and thunder brings your judgments forth.

The proud are cautioned not to boast,
the wicked, not to raise their eyes;
for you are king from east to west,
and you alone shall have the praise!

We come before you, God of gods—
your power shall cut the wicked down;
we worship you, the Lord of lords—
you lift us up to share your throne.

From Psalm 75.
Copyright © 1989 by Michael Perry/Jubilate Hymns Ltd.;
USA © 1989 by Hope Publishing Company, Carol Stream, IL 60188.

Tune: Cople/Paul Edwards or Winchester New/*Musikalisches Handbuch (1690)*—L.M.
(8.8.8.8.)

117.
O gracious Lord, be near me!
My soul cries out, 'How long?
When will you turn to hear me
and save your child from wrong?'

'How shall the voice you gave me
sing praises from the dead?
Return, O Lord, and save me;
in love lift up my head.'

I knew the fear of dying;
and sorrow filled my eyes;
but God who hears my crying,
in judgment will arise!

From Psalm 6.
Copyright © 1973 by Michael Perry/Jubilate Hymns Ltd.;
USA © 1973 by Hope Publishing Company, Carol Stream, IL 60188.

Tune: St Alphege/H J Gauntlett (1805-1876)—7.6.7.6.

118.

O Jesus my Lord, how sweetly you lie,
so far from home in heaven on high;
you come to do your Father's will,
to feel our pain, to cure our ill,
to live and serve, to love and die!

O Jesus my Lord, how sweetly you lie—
a helpless babe in poverty;
you deign to share our earthly fate,
and by your grace illuminate
the valley of our misery!

O Jesus my Lord, how sweetly you lie—
the Son revealed to human eye:
so light in us your flame of love
that we may lift our hearts above
to God, whom angels glorify!

O Jesus my Lord, how sweetly you lie
and show us God's humility:
accept the offering at our hands
of faithfulness to your commands,
and praise throughout eternity!

After S Scheidt (1587-1654).
Copyright © 1986 by Michael Perry/Jubilate Hymns Ltd.;
USA © 1986 by Hope Publishing Company, Carol Stream, IL 60188.

Tune: O Jesulein suss/Scheidt's *Tabulaturbuch* (1650)—10.9.8.8.8.

119.

O Lord, come quickly when I call,
receive my prayer with favor;
fair as the evening sacrifice,
as incense sweet to savor.

Keep watch upon my mouth, O Lord,
and guard my lips from evil;
so turn my heart from wicked ways
that I may shame the devil.

O Lord I'll seek your discipline—
but strengthen me to choose it;
your oil of grace anoints my head—
my head will not refuse it.

My eyes are fixed on you, O Lord,
though dangers yet surround me;
in life your love will be my rock,
and death shall not confound me.

From Psalm 141.
Copyright © 1989 by Michael Perry/Jubilate Hymns Ltd.;
USA © 1989 by Hope Publishing Company, Carol Stream, IL 60188.

Tune: Bugeilio'r Gwenith Gwyn/Welsh traditional melody or Dominus regit me/J B
Dykes (1823-1876)—8.7.8.7.

120.

O Lord, my rock, to you I cry
when others will not hear;
to you I lift my hands on high,
whose arms are always near.

I grieve for those who keep fine friends
but harbor Godless schemes;
who use your works for worthless ends,
to squander on their dreams.

Yet praise the Lord, who comes at length,
who comes to right the wrong;
to God our shepherd and our strength
be praise in joyful song!

From Psalm 28.
Copyright © 1989 by Michael Perry/Jubilate Hymns Ltd.;
USA © 1989 by Hope Publishing Company, Carol Stream, IL 60188.

Tune: St. Bernard, *Tochter Zion* Cologne (1741)—C.M. (8.6.8.6.)

121. *Variant*

O Lord, my rock, to you I cry
when others will not hear;
to you I lift my hands on high—
   your arms are always near, O Lord,
   your arms are always near.

I grieve for those who keep fine friends
but harbor Godless schemes;
who use your works for worthless ends,
   to squander on their dreams, O Lord,
   to squander on their dreams.

Yet praise the Lord, who comes at length,
who comes to right the wrong:
to you our shepherd and our strength
   be praise in joyful song, O Lord,
   be praise in joyful song!

From Psalm 28.
Copyright © 1989 by Michael Perry/Jubilate Hymns Ltd.;
USA © 1989 by Hope Publishing Company, Carol Stream, IL 60188.

Tune: Somerset/English traditional melody, or The Turtle Dove/English traditional
melody—8.6.8.8.6.

122.

O Lord, our Lord,
how wonderful
your name in all the earth!

Your greatness fills the skies,
the heavens tell your worth,
your children sing your praise
and set your glory forth:
    O Lord, our Lord,
    how wonderful
    your name in all the earth!

How great the moon and stars
that you have put in place!
And yet, as One who cares,
you meet us with your grace:
    O Lord, our Lord,
    how wonderful
    your name in all the earth!

You give into our care
the beasts of land and sea;
and all that fills the air
is ours by your decree:
    O Lord, our Lord,
    how wonderful
    your name in all the earth!

Sing glory to the Son
and to Father's name.
All, in the Spirit one,
the love of God proclaim:
    O Lord, our Lord,
    how wonderful
    your name in all the earth!

From Psalm 8.
Copyright © 1991 by Michael Perry/Jubilate Hymns Ltd.;
USA © 1991 by Hope Publishing Company, Carol Stream, IL 60188.

Tune: How wonderful/Michael Perry—6.6.6.6.Ref.

123.

O Lord, our Lord, your beauty fills the skies,
your name through all the earth is majesty:
from children's lips shall perfect praise arise
to silence every boasting enemy.

When I behold the worlds that you designed,
the moon and stars your fingers set in place,
I marvel that you care for humankind—
for honor made, in glory crowned with grace:

Through all the earth, across the spreading land,
upon the air and in the deepest sea,
we rule the creatures of your mighty hand—
O Lord, our Lord, your name is majesty!

From Psalm 8.
Copyright © 1989 by Michael Perry/Jubilate Hymns Ltd.;
USA © 1989 by Hope Publishing Company, Carol Stream, IL 60188.

Tune: Yanworth/John Barnard or Yardley Hastings/Paul Edwards—10.10.10.10.

124.

O Lord, the God who saves me,
to you my spirit cries;
my world is full of trouble,
all hope of mercy dies.

Your anger lies upon me,
I cannot make amends;
your waves, they overwhelm me,
you take away my friends.

And shall the dead sing praises,
and can the darkness see
your righteous ways, your wonders,
your faithfulness to me?

I call to you in waking,
and seek you all day long:
O hear me, Lord and Savior—
restore to me my song.

My God shall yet uplift me,
the Spirit come to save,
and Jesus my redeemer
shall meet me from the grave!

From Psalm 88.
Copyright © 1990 by Michael Perry/Jubilate Hymns Ltd.;
USA © 1990 by Hope Publishing Company, Carol Stream, IL 60188.

Tune: Blunham/Paul Edwards—7.6.7.6.

125.

O people, listen—hear God's wisdom crying!
Although the darkness comes to rich and poor,
and nothing mortal can survive our dying,
yet in the morning justice shall endure:

For God will take the holy into heaven,
by grace redeem the faithful from the grave;
we leave behind us all this world has given,
and trust God's mighty power to love and save!

To Father, Son and Spirit be the glory!
Come, worship and adore the holy Name;
let wisdom think upon our human story,
and faith our ever-living God proclaim.

From Psalm 49.
Copyright © 1989 by Michael Perry/Jubilate Hymns Ltd.;
USA © 1989 by Hope Publishing Company, Carol Stream, IL 60188.

Tune: Wharfdale/Michael Perry & Norman Warren or Highwood/R R Terry (1865-
1938)—11.10.11.10.

126.

O praise the Lord, the mighty God of Israel,
redeemer of his people he has come;
he raises up the dynasty of David
as promised by the prophets long ago.

Salvation from the hands of those who hate us!
His covenant with Abraham fulfilled!
He rescues us that, fearless, we might serve him
in honor and in goodness all our days.

And you will be the prophet of the Highest,
to go before him and prepare his way;
to give his people knowledge of salvation,
the blessing of forgiveness for their sins.

The Lord our God has shown his tender mercy,
the shining sun will come to us from heaven
to dawn on those who live in death's dark shadow,
and guide our footsteps in the path of peace.

Alternative first line:
O bless the Lord, the mighty God of Israel

From Luke 1 (Benedictus).
Copyright © 1990 by Michael Perry/Jubilate Hymns Ltd.;
USA © 1990 by Hope Publishing Company, Carol Stream, IL 60188.

Tune: Wharfdale/Michael Perry & Norman Warren—11.10.11.10.

127.

On a night when the world
    in its sin and sorrow lay,
the savior Jesus was born.

On a night when the world
    in its sin and sorrow lay,
close in a stall,
there the savior Jesus was born.

On a night when the world
    in its sin and sorrow lay,
in Bethlehem,
close in a stall,
there the savior Jesus was born.

On a night when the world
    in its sin and sorrow lay,
in Bethlehem,
close in a stall,
there the savior Jesus was born.

On a night when the world
    in its sin and sorrow lay,
on Christmas Day,
in Bethlehem,
close in a stall,
there the savior Jesus was born.

On a night when the world
    in its sin and sorrow lay,
'Peace on the earth!'—
on Christmas Day,
in Bethlehem,
close in a stall,
there the savior Jesus was born.

On a night when the world
    in its sin and sorrow lay,
angels were singing,
'Peace on the earth!'—
on Christmas Day,
in Bethlehem,
close in a stall,
there the savior Jesus was born.

On a night when the world
    in its sin and sorrow lay,
heavens were blazing,
angels were singing,
'Peace on the earth!'—
on Christmas Day,
in Bethlehem,
close in a stall,
there the savior Jesus was born.

On a night when the world
    in its sin and sorrow lay,
shepherds were watching,
heavens were blazing,
angels were singing,
'Peace on the earth!'—
On Christmas day,
in Bethlehem,
close in a stall,
there the savior Jesus was born.

On a night when the world
        in its sin and sorrow lay,
sheep were reclining,
shepherds were watching,
heavens were blazing,
angels were singing—
'Peace on the earth!'—
on Christmas Day,
in Bethlehem,
close in a stall,
there the savior Jesus was born.

On a night when the world
        in its sin and sorrow lay,
people were sleeping,
sheep were reclining,
shepherds were watching,
heavens were blazing,
angels were singing,
'Peace on the earth!'—
on Christmas Day,
in Bethlehem,
close in a stall,
there the savior Jesus was born.

On a night when the world
        in its sin and sorrow lay,
bright skies were shining,
people were sleeping,
sheep were reclining,
shepherds were watching,
heavens were blazing,
angels were singing,
'Peace on the earth!—
on Christmas Day,
in Bethlehem,
close in a stall,
there the savior Jesus was born.

On a night when the world
    in its sin and sorrow lay,
wise men were riding,
bright skies were shining,
people were sleeping,
sheep were reclining,
shepherds were watching,
heavens were blazing,
angels were singing,
'Peace on the earth!'—
on Christmas Day,
in Bethlehem,
close in a stall,
there the savior Jesus was born.

Tune: The Twelve days of Christmas/English traditional melody—Irregular

128.
One thing I know,
  that Christ has healed me—
though I was blind,
  yet now I see;
to him I owe,
  whose love has sealed me,
my heart and mind
  at last set free.

One thing I pray—
  that in my weakness,
God's perfect might
  will make me strong;
learning Christ's way
  whose selfless meekness
is my delight,
  my peace, my song.

One thing I do—
  put sin behind me,
press for the goal
  to win the prize;
for Christ I go
  who came to find me,
making me whole
  to gain the skies.

One faith, one Lord,
  one new creation,
one hope
  of our eternity!
One holy God!
  To our salvation,
glory and power
  for ever be!

Tune: Les Commandemens/ L Bourgeois (c1510-1651); Morar Murphy/Christopher
Rolinson—9.8.9.9.

129.

Only the fool will say
  'There is no God';
only the one whose way
  is full of lies:
and God looks down in vain
  to see their love,
for only few remain
  who do God's will.

Only from Zion shall
  salvation come;
only in God we all
  may live in peace:
lift high your voices, sing
  God's worthy praise,
and only serve your king
  who stoops to save.

From Psalm 53.
Copyright © 1990 by Michael Perry/Jubilate Hymns Ltd.;
USA © 1990 by Hope Publishing Company, Carol Stream, IL 60188.

Tune: Astwood/Paul Edwards—10.10.10.10.

130.

Praise him, praise him, praise him,
   powers and dominations;
praise his name in glorious light,
   you creatures of the day!
Moon and stars, ring praises
   through the constellations:
Lord God, whose word
   shall never pass away!

Praise him, praise him, praise him,
   ocean depths and waters;
elements of earth and heaven,
   your several praises blend!
Birds and beasts and cattle,
   Adam's sons and daughters,
worship the king
   whose reign shall never end!

Praise him, praise him, praise him,
   saints of God who fear him;
to the highest name of all,
   concerted anthems raise
all you seed of Israel,
   holy people near him—
whom he exalts
   and crowns with endless praise!

From Psalm 148.
Copyright © 1973 by Michael Perry/Jubilate Hymns Ltd.;
USA © 1973 by Hope Publishing Company, Carol Stream, IL 60188.

Tune: St. Helens/Kenneth Coates—12.13.13.10.

131.
Praise the Father, God of justice:
sinners tremble at his voice,
crowns and creatures fall before him,
saints triumphantly rejoice.

Praise the Son, who brings redemption,
purging sin and healing pain,
by whose cross and resurrection
we have died to rise again.

Praise the Spirit: power and wisdom,
peace that like a river flows,
word of Christ and consolation,
life by whom his body grows.

Praise the Father, Son and Spirit,
One-in-Three and Three-in-One,
God our Judge and God our Savior,
God our heaven on earth begun!

Tune: Stuttgart/C F Witt (1660-1716)—8.7.8.7.

132.
Rejoice with heart and voice!
Now is our Savior
of the virgin Mary born—
so rejoice!

At this time our God fulfills
all our expectation:
let us offer hearts and wills
in rededication.
Rejoice with heart and voice . . .

God of God when time began,
Lord of all creation:
we revere the Son of Man
at his incarnation.
Rejoice with heart and voice . . .

Alleluia! Let us sing
hymns of adoration,
blessing Christ our worthy king
in this celebration!
Rejoice with heart and voice . . .

From Gaudete.
Copyright © 1987 by Michael Perry/Jubilate Hymns Ltd.;
USA © 1987 by Hope Publishing Company, Carol Stream, IL 60188.

Tune: Gaudete/Medieval carol—Unique

133.

Ring, bells of Bethlehem,
   ding-dong-ding, ding-a-dong-a-ding;
rise up, Jerusalem,
joyfully sing.
Come from your lands afar,
   ding-dong-ding, ding-a-dong-a-ding,
follow the royal star,
look for the king!

Come, as the wise of old,
   ding-dong-ding, ding-a-dong-a-ding;
frankincense, myrrh and gold
joyfully bring:
incense shows fervent prayers,
   ding-dong-ding, ding-a-dong-a-ding,
myrrh his great love declares,
gold makes him king!

Ring, bells of Bethlehem,
   ding-dong-ding, ding-a-dong-a-ding;
rise up in Jerusalem,
joyfully sing.
Come and before him bow,
   ding-dong-ding, ding-a-dong-a-ding,
open your treasures now,
welcome your king!

Tune: English traditional melody—Unique

134.

Ring out the bells, and let the people know
that God is worshiped by the church below:
to all around this truth the bells declare—
'Your needs are lifted up to God in prayer!'

Ring out the bells, and let the people hear—
let hearts be open now, and faith draw near;
receive the grace that only God can give—
by word and symbol feed and grow and live.

Ring out the bells, and let the people sing
through changing seasons to our changeless King:
all perfect gifts are sent us from above—
respond with praises for such faithful love.

Ring out the bells until that glorious day
when death shall die and sin be done away:
then comes our God so everyone shall see—
let all the bells ring out in victory!

For the Dedication of the Eversley Bells.
Copyright © 1986 by Michael Perry/Jubilate Hymns Ltd.;
USA © 1986 by Hope Publishing Company, Carol Stream, IL 60188.

Tune: Wollaston/Paul Edwards or Yanworth/John Barnard or Woodlands/W
Greatorex—10.10.10.10.

135.
Ring out the bells—
the joyful news is breaking;
ring out the bells
for Jesus Christ is born!

Angels in wonder
sing of his glory;
shepherds returning
tell us the story.
Ring out the bells . . .

Let all creation
worship before him;
earth bring him homage,
heaven adore him!
Ring out the bells . . .

Prophets have spoken—
hark to their warning:
shadows are passing,
soon comes the morning!
Ring out the bells . . .

Tune: Past three a clock/English traditional melody—Unique

136.

Roar the waves, the waters praising
God who saves; and from beneath
creatures rise in shapes amazing
to our eyes—he gives them breath:
God who set the planets blazing
holds us yet in life or death.

Cries a bird at break of morning—
music heard when life began;
Christ was there at day's first dawning,
Son to share a Father's plan:
Jesus, born our hope and warning,
shall return—the Son of Man.

Sing the trees, the branches calling
in the breeze; the Spirit's song
sweeps the grass, the flowers falling,
Look! he passes all along;
wind of God whose strength appalling
mocks the proud and bends the strong.

Sound the praise of God the Father,
voices raise to Christ the Son;
in the Spirit Christians gather—
speak his merit everyone:
not in vain words glory—rather
tell again what God has done!

Tune: Triumph/H J Gauntlett (1805-1876)—8.7.8.7.8.7.

137.
Safe in the hands of God who made me,
what can there be that I should fear?
God is my light and my salvation,
strong is his help when foes are near.

This have I prayed and will seek after,
that I may walk with God each day;
then will he give me his protection,
no trouble shall my heart dismay.

God of my life, my Lord, my master,
father and mother now to me:
come, shield me from the threat of evil,
open your hands and set me free!

Teach me your way and lead me onwards,
save me from those who do me wrong;
give me the grace to wait with patience,
help me to trust, hold firm, be strong.

From Psalm 27.

Tune: by Christopher Norton—9.8.9.8.

138.

Save me, O God, hear my prayer,
open your ears to my cry;
keep me when evils prevail,
strengthen my hand from on high.

Yet shall the Lord be my help—
strong is the one who sustains;
offerings of love I will bring
God who eternally reigns.

From Psalm 54.
Copyright © 1989 by Michael Perry/Jubilate Hymns Ltd.;
USA © 1989 by Hope Publishing Company, Carol Stream, IL 60188.

Tune: Heather/Norman Warren, Knightwood/Hugh Benham—7.7.7.7.

139.
Savior Christ, in mercy come!
By your cross and life laid down
set your waiting people free—
come among us, Lord, today:

Come in power and loose our chains,
come in peace, forgive our sins,
come in truth to make us wise,
come and fill our hearts with praise:

Come to live among us, Lord—
come to save us by your word;
come today and make us one,
Savior Christ, in mercy come!

From Savior of the world.
Copyright © 1990 by Michael Perry and David Mowbray/Jubilate Hymns Ltd.;
USA © 1990 by Hope Publishing Company, Carol Stream, IL 60188.

Tune: Salvator mundi/David Llewellyn Green, Culbach/adapted from a chorale in J
Scheffler's *Heilige Seelenlust* Breslau 1657—7.7.7.7.

See him lying on a bed of straw

1 See him ly - ing on a bed of straw: a
2 Star of sil - ver, sweep a - cross the skies,
3 An - gels, sing a - gain the song you sang,
4 Mine are rich - es, from your pov - er - ty,

draf - ty sta - ble with an o - pen door;
show where Je - sus in the man - ger lies;
sing the glo - ry of God's gra - cious plan;
from your in - no-cence, e - ter - ni - ty;

Ma - ry cra - dl - ing the babe she bore – the
shep - herds, swift - ly from your stu - por rise to
sing that Beth - l'em's lit - tle ba - by can
mine for - give - ness by your death for me,

prince of glo - ry is his name.
see the sav - ior of the world!
be sal - va - tion to the soul.
child of sor - row for my joy.

Words: Michael Perry
Music: Michael Perry, arranged by Stephen Coates and others

Calypso Carol
9 9 9 7 and refrain

140.
See him lying on a bed of straw:
a drafty stable with an open door;
Mary cradling the babe she bore—
the prince of glory is his name.

    O now carry me to Bethlehem
    to see the Lord of love again:
    just as poor as was the stable then,
    the prince of glory when he came.

Star of silver, sweep across the skies,
show where Jesus in the manger lies;
shepherds, swiftly from your stupor rise
to see the savior of the world!

    O now carry . . .

Angels, sing again the song you sang,
sing the glory of God's gracious plan;
sing that Bethl'em's little baby can
be the saviour of us all.

    O now carry . . .

Mine are riches, from your poverty,
from your innocence, eternity;
mine, forgiveness by your death for me,
child of sorrow for my joy.

    O now carry . . .

Tune: Calypso Carol/Michael Perry—Irregular

141.
Shepherds, wake to news of joy—
  God's envoy
  comes to say
that for you is born a boy
close in David's town today!

Run to greet him—Christ the Lord,
  God's own Word,
  now arrayed
not with clothes the rich afford,
but in humble manger laid!

Hear the midnight angels' cry,
  through the sky
  ringing still:
'Glory be to God on high,
peace on earth—to all, goodwill;
peace on earth—to all, goodwill!'

Tune: The Fields of Bethlehem/Norman Warren—7.3.3.7.7.

142.

Shout aloud, girls and boys!
Sing today and rejoice,
lift your heart, raise your voice;
come, and do not waver,
God has shown us favor:
  virgin-born, born, born,
  virgin-born, born, born,
virgin-born, Mary's child,
Christ is here—our savior!

There you lie, Lord of all!
For your robe—peasant shawl,
for your bed—ox's stall,
for your throne a manger,
homeless as a stranger:
  come to win, win, win,
  come to win, win, win,
come to win hell's domain—
spurning death and danger!

Even now, from afar
wise men seek heaven's star,
bringing gifts where you are:
gold to bow before you,
incense to implore you,
  myrrh to say, say, say,
  myrrh to say, say, say,
myrrh to say 'sacrifice'—
therefore we adore you!

Boys and girls, voices raise!
Christmas choirs, sweetly phrase
songs of joy and of praise;
leave all care and worry,
sing the angels' story:
  Christ is born, born, born;
  Christ is born, born, born,
Christ is born, peace on earth—
and to God be glory!

From the Latin.
Copyright © 1986 by Michael Perry/Jubilate Hymns Ltd.;
USA © 1986 by Hope Publishing Company, Carol Stream, IL 60188.

Tune: Personent hodie/*Piae Cantiones* (1852)—6.6.6.6.6.5.5.6.6.

143.

Silver star
  shining out over Bethlehem,
lead worshipers from afar,
  inspiring and guiding them!
They look for the infant King—
  with their gifts they will honor him;
and love in their hearts they bring,
  true service to offer him.

Holy night
  for a pilgrim to journey through!
O traveler, seek the light
  that welcomes and beckons you!
You come to the brink of heaven,
  to the gateway of paradise;
for you has the Child been given,
  on you shall the Sun arise.

Silent sky
  full of wonder and mystery—
the splendor of God most high,
  the mantle of majesty!
Yet God lays aside his crown—
  O give praise to the mighty Lord!
and for our release comes down—
  O welcome the living Word!

Tune: Polovtsian Dance/Borodin—Unique

144.

Sing to the Lord
with a song of profound delight,
serve him by day
and bring praises in the night:

MEN   tell of the battles fought for us

A   marvelous

B   glorious

WOMEN   tell of his wonders done for us,

ALL   worthy of acclaim.

Beauty and power
are the marks of our Savior's grace,
splendor and light
shine in glory from his face:

MEN   worship the Lord in holiness,

A   faithfulness,

B   godliness—

WOMEN   judging the world
with righteousness

ALL   he will come to reign.

So let the skies sing aloud
and the earth rejoice—
beasts of the field
and the forest lift their voice:

MEN   firmly he set the solid ground,

A   seas abound,

B   skies resound;

WOMEN   all we desire in God is found—

ALL   glory to his name!

The singers may divide at A and B.

From Psalm 96.
Copyright © 1990 by Michael Perry/Jubilate Hymns Ltd.;
USA © 1990 by Hope Publishing Company, Carol Stream, IL 60188.

Tune: Marche Militaire (1)/F. Schubert (1797-1828)—Unique

145.

Sleep, Lord Jesus! Mary smiling
on her infant so beguiling
   sings a joyful lullaby.

Sleep, Lord Jesus! Mary grieving
at the fate our sin is weaving
   sings a solemn lullaby.

Sleep, Lord Jesus! Mary dreaming
of this fallen world's redeeming
   sings a holy lullaby.

Sleep, Lord Jesus, Lullaby!

Based on the Latin.
Copyright © 1986 by Michael Perry/Jubilate Hymns Ltd.;
USA © 1986 by Hope Publishing Company, Carol Stream, IL 60188.

Tune: Dormi Jesu/Tom Cunningham—8.8.7.

146.
Soldiers marching
   ta-rata-ta-ta
the streets of Bethlehem,
   ta-rata-ta-ta
a little king to find
   ta-rata-ta-ta
for Herod's peace of mind,
   ta-rata-ta-ta
   rata-ta-ta, rata-ta-ta
since the wise men spoke
   ta rata-ta-ta
of a star.

Soldiers knocking
   ta-rata-ta-ta
on doors of Bethlehem,
   ta-rata-ta-ta.
obeying Herod's will
   ta-rata-ta-ta
all infant boys to kill,
   ta-rata-ta-ta
   rata-ta-ta, rata-ta-ta
paying well to know
   ta-rata-ta-ta
where they are.

Soldiers marching
 ta-rata-ta-ta
away from Bethlehem,
 ta-rata-ta-ta
despising mothers' cries,
 ta-rata-ta-ta
to Herod telling lies:
 ta-rata-ta-ta,
 rata-ta-ta, rata-ta-ta
Jesus whom they seek
 ta-rata-ta-ta
is afar.

Tune: Carol of the Drum/Harry Simeone and Henty Onorati—Unique

147.
Songs of gladness,
songs of gladness,
  let us sing,
  let us sing!
Glory to our savior,
glory to our savior
  and our king
  and our king!

Joyful tidings,
joyful tidings,
  ring, bells, ring;
  ring, bells, ring!
Sound aloud his praises,
sound aloud his praises:
  Ding-dong, ding,
  ding-dong, ding!

Copyright © 1997 by Michael Perry/Jubilate Hymns Ltd.;
USA © 1997 by Hope Publishing Company, Carol Stream, IL 60188.

Tune: Frère Jacques/French traditional melody—Unique

148.

Sovereign Lord, in all the earth
how majestic is your name!
Infant voices from their birth
  fervent praise proclaim.

When I lift my eyes I see
all the stars you set in place:
who am I that I should be
  favored by such grace?

Yet you prove to us your love
and exalt us very high,
making us as lords above
  earth and sea and sky.

Sing aloud our savior's worth—
mercy, truth and love proclaim:
Sovereign Lord, in all the earth
  holy is your name!

From Psalm 8.
Copyright © 1990 by Michael Perry/Jubilate Hymns Ltd.;
USA © by Hope Publishing Company, Carol Stream, IL 60188.

Tune: by Chris Rolinson (with last line repeat)—7.7.7.5.

149.

Surely God the Lord is good,
    guiding all those whose hearts are pure;
at God's hands we take our food,
    in God's love we are secure:
vainly do the heathen cry,
    'Can the Most High watch us all?'
Shamed by that all-seeing eye,
    soon the boasting proud will fall.

When my stumbling footsteps tire,
    strengthen me in all I do—
earth has no more I desire;
    whom have I in heaven but you?
Though my flesh and heart shall fail,
    you supply immortal needs;
with your help I shall prevail
    and proclaim your perfect deeds.

Yes, this earth-bound fantasy
    shall disperse when you arise;
when you come to welcome me
    to your home beyond the skies.
Glory be to God today,
    every heart by grace forgiven;
souls redeemed and angels say,
    Glory in the highest heaven!

From Psalm 73.
Copyright © 1990 by Michael Perry/Jubilate Hymns Ltd.;
USA © 1990 by Hope Publishing Company, Carol Stream, IL 60188.

Tune: Calon Lân/J Hughes (1873-1932)—7.7.7.7.D.

150.

The brightness of God's glory
  and the image of God's being,
the heir of richest majesty,
  the arm of regal might;
creator of the universe
  all-knowing and all-seeing
is Christ who brings forgiveness
  and the lifting of our night.

Far greater than the angels
  is the author of salvation,
begotten of his Father's love
  before all time began:
our offering of righteousness,
  our refuge from temptation,
one hope in all our sufferings
  is Christ, the Son of Man.

How awesome is his perfect life
  unending and unbroken,
how faultless are his judgments
  and how faithful is his word!
Then hear, repent and worship him,
  obey, for God has spoken,
receive the Holy Spirit
  and acknowledge Christ as Lord!

From Hebrews 1.
Copyright © 1982 by Michael Perry/Jubilate Hymns Ltd.;
USA © 1982 by Hope Publishing Company, Carol Stream, IL 60188.

Tune: Rootham's Green/Paul Edwards—15.14.15.14.

151.

The God of heaven thunders,
whose voice in strident echoes
resounds above the waters—
and all the world sings,
   Glory, glory, glory!

The desert writhes in tempest,
wind whips the trees to fury,
the lightning splits the forest—
and flame diffuses
   glory, glory, glory.

The mighty God eternal
is to the throne ascended,
and we who are God's people,
within these walls cry:
   Glory, glory, glory!

From Psalm 29.
Copyright © 1973 by Michael Perry/Jubilate Hymns Ltd.;
USA © 1973 by Hope Publishing Company, Carol Stream, IL 60188.

Tune: Glory/Norman Warren—7.7.7.11.

The hands of Christ

With a gentle lilt ♩. = 60

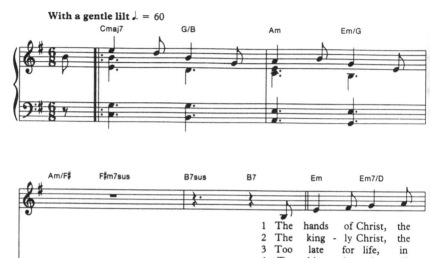

1 The hands of Christ, the
2 The king - ly Christ, the
3 Too late for life, in
4 To him be praise, all

car - ing hands, they nailed them to a
sav - iour - king, they hailed him with a
death too late they tried to maim him
praise to him who died up - on the

Words: Michael Perry
Music: Michael Perry, arranged by David Peacock

Beatrice
8 8 8 4

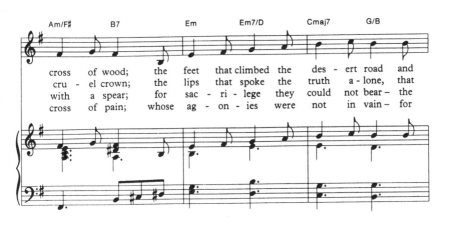

Am/F#	B7	Em	Em7/D	Cmaj7	G/B	

cross of wood; the feet that climbed the des - ert road and
cru - el crown; the lips that spoke the truth a - lone, that
with a spear; for sac - ri - lege they could not bear — the
cross of pain; whose ag - on - ies were not in vain — for

Am7	Dsus	D/F#	G	Em

brought the news of peace with God, they
made the way to hea - ven known, they
sab - bath comes, so they must tear the
Christ the Lord is risen a - gain and

Am/F#	F#dim/B	1–3. Em	Em/D	4. Em

pierced them through._____
mocked with wine._____
heart from God._____
brings us joy!_____

152.

The hands of Christ, the caring hands,
they nailed them to a cross of wood;
the feet that climbed the desert road
and brought the news of peace with God,
    they pierced them through.

The kingly Christ, the savior-king,
they ringed his head with briars woven;
the lips that freely spoke of heaven,
that told the world of sins forgiven,
    they mocked with wine.

Too late for life, in death too late,
they tried to maim him with a spear;
for sacrilege they could not bear—
the sabbath comes, so they must tear
    the heart from God.

To him be praise, all praise to him
who died upon the cross of pain;
whose agonies were not in vain—
for Christ the Lord is risen again
    and brings us joy!

Alternative second verse—to assist with meter when sung:
    The kingly Christ, the savior-king,
    they hailed him with a cruel crown;
    the lips that spoke the truth alone,
    that made the way to heaven known,
        they mocked with wine.

Tune: Beatrice/Michael Perry, Medfield Street/Simon Beckley—8.8.8.7.

153.

The majesty of mountains,
the sovereignty of skies,
the regal rocks that arch above
where veils of vapor rise,
are gifts of God, the Lord of love,
the worshipful, the wise.

The running of the river,
the surging of the sea,
the grass that grows high on the hill,
the flower and fruiting tree,
our Savior sends us, by whose will
all creatures came to be.

The glory of the Godhead,
the Spirit and the Son,
the Father, faithful down the days:
to them, the Three-in-One,
while life shall last be perfect praise
and highest honor done!

From Psalm 104, for the family Von Rad.
Copyright © 1987 by Michael Perry/Jubilate Hymns Ltd.;
USA © 1987 by Hope Publishing Company, Carol Stream, IL 60188.

Tune: Eythorne/John Barnard or Misterioso/Christopher Norton—7.6.8.6.8.6.

154.

The story has broken,
an angel has spoken,
and this is the token
    that Jesus is here:
he comes as a stranger
regardless of danger,
the Lord in a manger,
    the babe without peer.

Oh counsel of splendor,
oh sacrifice tender,
that God should surrender
    to us in this way—
his purpose revealing,
his promises sealing,
the pledge of our healing,
    the dawn of our day!

The shepherds returning,
and wise men of learning,
their savior discerning,
    his praises will sing:
as those who first saw him
and knelt down before him,
so let us adore him
    and worship our king.

Oh infinite treasure,
oh love without measure—
it is God's good pleasure
    to give us his Son,
the source of creation,
the hope of each nation,
the great jubilation
    of heaven begun!

Tune: The Ash Grove/English traditional melody—6.6.6.5.D.

155.

There's a bright sky over Bethlehem,
where shepherds watch upon the hill:
   and the heavens ring
   as angels sing
of peace on earth and God's goodwill!

There's a savior come to Bethlehem,
a baby laid upon the hay:
   in a stable bare
   no comfort where
the Christ is born this holy day.

There's a star high over Bethlehem—
the wise men start upon the road:
   bearing gold and myrrh
   and incense rare
they come to find the Son of God.

There's a sign for us in Bethlehem,
for we rejoice at Christmastide
   to receive our Lord,
   God's living Word,
our love, our light, our friend, our guide!

Tune: Marloes/Roger Mayor—6.6.6.5.D.

156.

To God's loving kindness
  we commit you:
the Lord bless your life
    and make you strong—
    may the praises of God,
    the Father and the Son
    and the Spirit—Three-in-One,
be your song.

To God's holy favor
  we commend you:
the Lord hear your prayers
    and show his face—
    and the mercy of God,
    the Father and the Son
    and the Spirit—Three-in-One,
bring you grace.

To God's great protection
  we entrust you:
the Lord take your hand
    and give you peace—
    let the blessing of God,
    the Father and the Son
    and the Spirit—Three-in-One,
never cease!

From Numbers 6.
Copyright © 1982 by Michael Perry/Jubilate Hymns Ltd.;
USA © 1982 by Hope Publishing Company, Carol Stream, IL 60188.

Tune: Oakley/Michael Perry—10.9.6.6.10.

157.
To lead a blameless life, O Lord,
to trust you without fear,
to bring my humble heart to you
and know your love is near:

To walk before you in the truth,
to shun all evil ways,
to come into your house to pray
and shout aloud your praise:

Let this be my supreme desire,
my object and my prayer,
until I stand before your throne
to glorify you there!

From Psalm 26.
Copyright © 1989 by Michael Perry/Jubilate Hymns Ltd.;
USA © 1989 by Hope Publishing Company, Carol Stream, IL 60188.

Tune: Talbot Woods/Michael Dawney—C.M. (8.6.8.6.)

158.

To those who rule our land,
give justice, love and truth;
Lord, help them to defend the poor,
to keep us safe, to guard the law,
and prosper at your hand:

Let mercy all their days
fall as refreshing showers;
Lord, guide the people with your light
that we may flourish in your sight,
and earth be filled with praise!

From Psalm 72.
Copyright © 1989 by Michael Perry/Jubilate Hymns Ltd.;
USA © 1989 by Hope Publishing Company, Carol Stream, IL 60188.

Tune: Maiden Way/E Routley (1917-1982)—6.6.8.8.6.

159.

To your praise, O God almighty,
    Israel's holy Lord and ours,
be ascribed, through all the ages,
    victories, dominions, powers!
Maker of the earth and heaven,
    master of the sea and land:
none made low without your pleasure,
    none raised up but by your hand.

Now enthroned above in triumph,
    Christ who lives, who once was slain;
ransomed hosts from every nation
    risen with Christ, with Christ shall reign:
for the Lamb of God, is worthy
    to receive through endless days
from all creatures, honour, glory,
    power, wisdom, might and praise.

Countless thousands in the heavens,
    on the earth and in the sea
fall before the Godhead crying:
    'Blessing, honour, victory—
great and marvellous are your wonders,
    just and perfect are your ways!'
Come, all heaven and earth, adoring—
    bring to God eternal praise!

From 1 Chronicles 29 and Revelation 4-5
Copyright © 1983 by Michael Perry/Jubilate Hymns Ltd.;
USA © 1983 by Hope Publishing Company, Carol Stream, IL 60188.

Tune: Hyfrydol/R H Prichard (1811-1887)—8.7.8.7.D.

160.
We are a world divided—
unworthy of you, Lord;
and yet by your great mercy
our peace can be restored:

Though we invite your anger
and fail to do your will,
yet if we turn and fear you
your love can triumph still.

Our God is strong to save us
and tread the evil down,
to raise the cause of justice
and gain the victor's crown.

Sing glory to the Father,
bring worship to the Son,
adore the Holy Spirit:
praise God the Three-in-One. (Amen).

[*Stanza 1 alternative:*
We are a land divided . . .]

From Psalm 60.
Copyright © 1989 by Michael Perry/Jubilate Hymns Ltd.;
USA © 1989 by Hope Publishing Company, Carol Stream, IL 60188.

Tune: Potterne/John Barnard, Aurelia/S S Wesley (1810-1876)—7.6.7.6.D.

161.

We give God thanks for those who knew
the touch of Jesus' healing love;
they trusted him to make them whole,
to give them peace, their guilt remove.

We offer prayer for all who go
relying on God's grace and power,
to help the anxious and the ill,
to heal their wounds, their lives restore.

We dedicate our skills and time
to those who suffer where we live,
to bring such comfort as we can
to meet their need, their pain relieve.

So, Jesus' touch of healing grace
lives on within our willing care;
by thought and prayer and gifts we prove
his mercy still, his love we share.

Tune: Melcombe/S Webbe the elder (1740-1816) or Newinnton/Colin Avery—L.M.
(8.8.8.8.)

162.

We hail the approaching God,
who quickly comes from heaven,
and celebrate with festive songs
such love so freely given.

Within a virgin's womb
he hides his liberty;
the immortal Lord becomes a slave
to set his people free.

O run to greet your king
who stands on Zion's hill:
to all who hear his word of peace,
his arms are stretched out still.

Soon, shining in the cloud,
the Lord will come again
and take his Body to the skies
to live and love and reign.

Then night and death shall yield,
and sin be done away;
then Adam shall be made anew
on that tremendous day.

To Father, Spirit, Son,
the God whom we adore,
be highest praise and honor now,
and glory evermore!

After C Coffin (1676-1749).
Copyright © 1986 by Michael Perry/Jubilate Hymns Ltd.;
USA © 1986 by Hope Publishing Company, Carol Stream, IL 60188.

Tune: St. Thomas/A Williams' *New Universal Psalmodist* (1770)—S.M. (6.6.8.6.)

163.

We have heard, O Lord our God
the story of your grace; ·
and how you gave to us this land,
defending us with your right hand
and showing us your face.

You are great, O Lord our God,
we trusted in your name;
we did not triumph by the sword,
but through the victory of your word
you put our foes to shame.

Yet, today O Lord our God,
the weak—who once were strong—
cry out to you, 'O come, arise,
reveal your light to darkened eyes,
and turn our sighs to song!'

From Psalm 44.
Copyright © 1989 by Michael Perry/Jubilate Hymns Ltd.;
USA © 1989 by Hope Publishing Company, Carol Stream, IL 60188.

Tune: Great Glen/Peter White—7.6.8.8.6.

164.

We lift our hearts up to the Lord—
who stoops to hear us praying;
and as we wait upon his word,
we find in Jesus our reward
all other joys outweighing.

As every passing day we move
upon the world's procession,
however dark the way may prove,
we'll seek the light of Jesus' love,
his peace as our possession.

Through pain and laughter, smiles and tears—
from youth's high aspiration,
to wisdom after many years,
he speaks of hope to listening ears:
'Rejoice in my salvation!'

When, overcast, the skies bode ill,
the trees suspend their motion,
the last birds' cries are strangely shrill,
we'll lift my heart to Jesus still
in worship and devotion.

Tune: none as yet—8.7.8.8.7.

165.

We share a new day's dawn with Christ,
our lives refreshed, our hopes restored:
this is the day to serve our Lord!
And with this new day's dawn we rise
and lift our hearts up to the skies.

For heaven's grace we turn to prayer,
for truth and strength we read Christ's word:
here is the grace to serve our Lord!
And so by heaven's grace this day
we'll learn to walk in Jesus' way.

Our song shall be of perfect love—
of Christ's redemption, faith's reward:
this is love's service to our Lord!
And perfect love shall be our song
till all our days to Christ belong.

Tune: Pachelbe (Was Gott thut)/*Nürnberg Gesangbuch*—8.8.8.8.8. Also *Nessum Dorma* (see commentary)

166.

We thank you, God, for feeding us
in Jesus Christ our Lord:
his body broken is our food,
our life, his cleansing blood.

Through him we offer you ourselves—
our all, to be your own;
a holy, living sacrifice
to lay before your throne.

So send us out into the world
your glory to proclaim,
and in your Holy Spirit's power
to live and praise your name.

From the Prayer of Thanksgiving After Communion, the Anglican *Alternative Service Book 1980*
Copyright © 1992 by Michael Perry/Jubilate Hymns Ltd.;
USA © 1992 by Hope Publishing Company, Carol Stream, IL 60188.

Tune: Bishopthorpe/Josiah Clarke (c.1674-1707); Dundee (French)/*Scottish Psalter* Edinburgh 1615—C.M. (8.6.8.6.)

167.

We will tell each generation
all that you, our God, have done;
how you called and led our nation,
chose us out to be your own:

Tell the times of our rebelling—
how we wandered from your way,
how your law our love compelling
taught us humbly to obey:

Tell how once, when spite and terror
threatened to engulf our land,
you defended us with vigor,
saved us by a mighty hand:

Tell the grace that falls from heaven,
angels' food as faith's reward;
tell how sins may be forgiven
through the mercy of the Lord.

From Psalm 78.
Copyright © 1989 by Michael Perry/Jubilate Hymns Ltd.;
USA © 1989 by Hope Publishing Company, Carol Stream, IL 60188.

Tune: Restoration/*The Southern Harmony (1835)* or Stuttgart/C F Witt (1660-1716)—8.7.8.7.

168.

Welcome, Child of Mary,
    coming from above—
our visitor from heaven,
    our Lord of love!
Jesus, dearest savior,
all praise is yours by right,
now returned to glory,
beyond our human sight.
    Have mercy, Lord!

Shepherds in the pasture
    hearing angels sing,
receive with joy and wonder
    the news they bring:
'Go to seek your savior;
now swiftly make your way—
you will surely find him
in Bethlehem today!'
    Have mercy, Lord!

Wise men from the orient,
    skilled to understand
the star that lights the heavens
    their eyes have scanned:
soon they find the savior
and bring him presents rare,
who can keep our treasure
secure within his care.
    Have mercy, Lord!

From the Dutch.
Copyright © 1987 by Michael Perry/Jubilate Hymns Ltd.;
USA © 1987 by Hope Publishing Company, Carol Stream, IL 60188.

Tune: Nu zijt wellekome/15th Century Dutch melody—Unique

169.
Welcome, Jesus child of Mary,
David's son and Judah's star!
  Alleluia, alleluia,
  alleluia, gloria!

Welcome, Jesus child of Mary,
come to us from realms afar—
  Alleluia . . .

Tune: O du fröliche/Sicilian folk melody—8.7.8.7.

170.
Welcome, welcome,
savior come to Bethlehem;
'Glory, glory',
heaven's angels say:
Welcome, welcome—
we shall join to sing with them,
'Glory, glory:
Christ is born today!'

Welcome, welcome,
God in our humanity;
Glory, glory,
praise him and adore:
welcome, welcome,
spurning princely vanity,
Glory, glory,
God among the poor.

Welcome, welcome—
lift your voices, everyone;
Glory, glory,
sing with glad acclaim:
Welcome, welcome,
welcome God's belovèd Son;
Glory, glory,
glory to his name!

Tune: by Norman Warren—11.9.11.9.

171.

When God from heaven to earth came down
  on Christmas Day, on Christmas Day,
the songs rang out in Bethlehem town
  on Christmas Day in the morning.

For Christ was born to save us all,
  on Christmas Day, on Christmas Day,
and laid within a manger stall
  on Christmas Day in the morning.

The shepherds heard the angels sing
  on Christmas Day, on Christmas Day,
to tell them of the savior-king
  on Christmas Day in the morning.

Now joy is ours and all is well,
  on Christmas Day, on Christmas Day,
so sound the organ, chime the bell
  on Christmas Day in the morning.

Tune: I saw three ships/English traditional—L.M. (8.8.8.8.)

172.

When I lift up my voice,
and I cry for your help,
and I pour out my troubles before you:
I say:
   You are my refuge,
   and I will praise your name;
   you are good to me, O Lord!

When I see no-one cares,
and I walk all alone,
and my spirit grows weary within me:
I say:
   You are my refuge . . .

When you come to my side
and you answer my prayers,
and you set my soul free from its prison:
I say:
   You are my refuge . . .

Variant: 'When I lift up my voice'

From Psalm 142.
Copyright © 1990 by Michael Perry/Jubilate Hymns Ltd.;
USA © 1990 by Hope Publishing Company, Carol Stream, IL 60188.

Tunes: You are my refuge (John Barnard), by Christopher Norton, by Michael Perry,
and by Chris Rolinson—Irregular

173.
When I'm afraid
  I will trust in God,
when I'm afraid I will say,
'What can anyone do to me—
  God is mine today?'

When I'm alone
  I will ask God's help,
when I'm alone I will pray:
how can anyone spoil my peace—
  I am God's today?

While I'm alive
  I will speak God's praise.
while I'm alive I will sing:
who can any more come between
  me and God my king?

From Psalm 56.
Copyright © 1900 by Michael Perry/Jubilate Hymns Ltd.;
USA © 1990 by Hope Publishing Company, Carol Stream, IL 60188.

Tune: Silverdale/Brian Hoare—8.8.8.7.

174.

When Jesus Christ was eight days old
they named him as they had been told;
name of our saviour and our Lord,
spoken to Mary—Gabriel's word.

And when the proper time had come,
they took him to Jerusalem;
there in the temple court they prayed
and for the boy an offering made.

'Lord, let this child be all your own,
and in his life your will be done!'
And on that day, before he died
the agéd Simeon prophesied:

'Now let your servant go in peace:
these eyes have seen your saving grace;
a light to lighten all the world—
the joy of heaven, the Son of God!'

From Luke 2.
Copyright © 1993 by Michael Perry/Jubilate Hymns Ltd.;
USA © 1993 by Hope Publishing Company, Carol Stream, IL 60188.

Tune: Peter Ilich Tcaikovsky (1840-1893)—L.M. (8.8.8.8.)

175.

When Jesus walked upon this earth
his word was peace;
he spoke of fellowship with God,
he brought the prisoners release;
and all his caring
witnessed to his peaceful word.

When Jesus walked upon the earth
his touch was grace;
they came with stretcher and with crutch
from east and west to seek his face;
and all his healing
witnessed to his gracious touch.

When Jesus walked upon this earth
his heart was love;
he came to take the humblest part,
among the penitent to move;
and all his serving
witnessed to his loving heart.

When Jesus walked upon this earth
they named him 'king';
to fight demonic powers he came
and bring his glorious kingdom in:
let all our praising
witness to his kingly name!

Tune: Thurleigh/Paul Edwards—8.4.8.8.5.7.

176.

When my bitter foes surround,
when their wicked deeds confound,
when deceit and lies abound,
 I will hope in God.

When deep sorrows overpower,
when lies hurt and doubts devour,
when I face my darkest hour,
 I will trust in God.

Then shall fervent prayers avail,
then shall light and truth prevail,
then God's mercy will not fail:
 I will praise my God.

From Psalm 43.
Copyright © 1990 by Michael Perry/Jubilate Hymns Ltd.;
USA © 1990 by Hope Publishing Company, Carol Stream, IL 60188.

Tune: Carsaig/G Thalben-Ball (1896-1987)—7.7.7.5.

177.

When shepherds watched and angels sang
and Judah's hills with glory rang,
then Christ was born the Son of Man
on Christmas Day in the morning:
   Christ was born the Son of Man
   on Christmas Day, on Christmas Day;
   Christ was born the Son of Man
   on Christmas Day in the morning.

When Joseph knelt and Mary bowed
and beasts of burden brayed aloud,
there Christ was born for all our good
on Christmas Day in the morning:
   Christ was born for all our good
   on Christmas Day, on Christmas Day;
   Christ was born for all our good
   on Christmas Day in the morning.

When wise men sought and Herod feared
and when a royal star appeared,
then Christ was born to be our Lord
on Christmas Day in the morning:
   Christ was born to be our Lord
   on Christmas Day, on Christmas Day;
   Christ was born to be our Lord
   on Christmas Day in the morning.

Where God no longer calls in vain
and human hearts are love's domain,
there Christ is born in us again
on Christmas Day in the morning:
   Christ is born in us again
   on Christmas Day, on Christmas Day;
   Christ is born in us again
   on Christmas Day in the morning.

Copyright © 1987 by Michael Perry/Jubilate Hymns Ltd.;
USA © 1987 by Hope Publishing Company, Carol Stream, IL 60188.

Tune: Greensleeves/English traditional melody—Unique

178.

When the angel came to Mary
he said, 'Be at peace,
for the Lord God shall be with you,
his love will not cease.'
   And Mary bore Jesus Christ,
   our savior for to be;
   and the first and the last
   and the greatest is he, is he, is he;
   and the first and the last
   and the greatest is he.

When the angel came to Mary
he said, 'Do not fear,
for his power shall be upon you,
a child you will bear.'
   And Mary bore Jesus Christ . . .

When the angel came to Mary
he said, 'Hear his name,
for his title shall be Jesus
of kingly acclaim.'
   And Mary bore Jesus Christ . . .

When the angel came to Mary,
she said, 'Be it so;
for the Lord God is my master,
his will I must do.'
   And Mary bore Jesus Christ . . .

After the traditional carol.
Copyright © 1986 by Michael Perry/Jubilate Hymns Ltd.;
USA © 1986 by Hope Publishing Company, Carol Stream, IL 60188.

Tune: Sans Day Carol/Cornish traditional melody—Unique

179.

When the waters cover me,
    save me, O God;
when I look and cannot see,
when I seek what cannot be,
when my friends abandon me,
    save me, O God.

You know all my guilty fears,
    thank you, O God,
you have heard with open ears,
you have seen my contrite tears,
you will bless me all the years—
    thank you, O God.

From Psalm 69.
(See also 'When my sorrows cover me')
Copyright © 1989 by Michael Perry/Jubilate Hymns Ltd.;
USA © 1989 by Hope Publishing Company, Carol Stream, IL 60188.

Tune: Salvum me/David Llewellyn Green—7.4.7.7.7.4.

180.
When we walk with God, we are blessed:
    not the wicked or their schemes,
    nor the evil and their dreams—
when we walk with God,
    we are blessed.

When we trust in God, we are blessed:
    when his law is our delight,
    and we heed it day and night—
when we trust in God,
    we are blessed.

When we feed on God, we are blessed:
    like a growing tree in place
    by the flowing stream of grace—
when we feed on God,
    we are blessed.

When we walk with God, we are blessed:
    for the Lord is at our side
    our redeemer and our guide—
when we walk with God,
    we are blessed.

From Psalm 1
Copyright © 1990 by Michael Perry/Jubilate Hymns Ltd.;
USA © 1990 by Hope Publishing Company, Carol Stream, IL 60188.

Tune: by Chris Rolinson—8.7.7.8.

181.
Who can bind the raging sea
  or walk the ocean floor?
Who can find where snow is made,
  or hail is kept in store?
Who can know how light begins
  or darkness ends the day?
Who can go where planets grow,
  or show someone the way?

Who directs the rushing stream
  and steers the rolling storm?
Who protects the lion cubs
  and ravens' young from harm?
Who decides when deer shall breed
  or mountain goats give birth?
Who provides, defends and guides?
  The Lord of all the earth!

In God's hands the awesome power
  that hurls the stars through space:
God commands—the lightning strikes,
  the thunderclouds embrace!
God's arm flings the waters high
  and trims the foam-flecked waves;
Glory, sing to heaven's king—
  our God who loves and saves!

From Job 38 and 39.
Copyright © 1989 by Michael Perry/Jubilate Hymns Ltd.;
USA © 1989 by Hope Publishing Company, Carol Stream, IL 60188.

Tune: none as yet—7.6.7.6.D.

182.

Who is this child that lies in humble splendor,
and spurns the night and braves the winter wild?
Was ever babe so lowly and so tender,
yet full of grace? Who is this little child?
   This is the Christ, in whom we are forgiven;
   this is the Lord, the mighty Son of Man;
   this is our God,
      who comes to us from heaven—
   the living Word
      who was before the world began!

What shall we sing to celebrate his story,
to praise our Lord and glorify our king?
How shall we tell the people of his glory,
and share his grace? What shall his people sing?
   This is the Christ . . .

Tune: Londonderry Air/Irish traditional melody—11.10.11.10.11.10.11.12.

183.

You laid the foundations of earth,
the heavens were wrought by your hands;
they perish, but you will remain,
they falter, but your glory stands.

Like clothing the worlds shall be changed,
the skies cast away like a veil;
but you, Lord, are always the same,
your years like your words never fail.

Your servants shall trust in your love,
our children shall walk in your ways,
till time holds us captive no more
and paradise rings with your praise!

From Psalm 102.
Copyright © 1989 by Michael Perry/Jubilate Hymns Ltd.;
USA © 1989 by Hope Publishing Company, Carol Stream, IL 60188.

Tune: Grendon/Paul Edwards; Limburg/David Iliff—L.M. (8.8.8.8.)

APPENDIX

In 1972 a mother came to me for comfort for her little girl who had recently lost a child friend to cancer. I wrote this poem for the girl in the hope that she would glimpse the understanding we have through the cross of Jesus. It is not intended as a hymn, but I felt that my collection would not be complete without it. MP.

For Emma

Now, sometimes God has strange ideas,
and I just wonder why
he shouldn't think it horrible
that little children die,
and that the nicest folk have hurts,
and that the hungry cry.

I hear them say 'It's for the best',
they tell me, 'God is love';
as if it looked a different way
when seen from up above.
But if it's true that God loves all,
then how *can* he approve?

I often ask if God is deaf
or if he's really there—
I reckon he's had more than time
to think about my prayer.
Our Father, will you do something,
or don't you really care?

By all accounts, he's strong enough—
he rules the land and sea,
he flings the planets into space
and sets volcanoes free.
But can he stop this suffering?
He can't, it seems to me.

Perhaps I shouldn't talk like this;
I ought to hold my tongue.
Perhaps there's some mistake I've made—
I must have got it wrong.
Perhaps the answer to my prayer
has been there all along.

Now, Jesus Christ of Nazareth,
in Israel's far-off land:
It's when I come to look at you
I start to understand,
and in my fear and puzzlement
I reach out for your hand.

O caring Jesus, kind and good,
you died when you were young;
that God in you might share our pain,
you mourned and grieved and clung
to sorrow on a wooden cross,
and blessed us as you hung.

So, God has suffered, too, you see;
he did not stand outside
in comfort while we sorrowed here
but, just like us, he cried
to see his friends so badly ill
and, as we must, he died.

And this I know, from Easter Day:
that evil cannot win;
that Christ removes our guiltiness,
and God forgives our sin.
For heaven's gate is open wide
and, one day, we'll go in.

There are so many people still
who haven't learned to pray;
so few have heard that God is real,
and need to know. One day
I'll tell them all how much he cares,
and this is what I'll say:

That Jesus suffers when we do,
that just like us he cries,
that Jesus looks upon the world
with sad and feeling eyes.
But then, he makes this promise too—
that we, in him, shall rise.

Information—Hymn text commentary

1.

A child is born in Bethlehem

This is based on translation from a Danish original by Ester Jensen of Kibæk in Jutland. The Danish carol is sung to a sixteenth century German melody, eventually published with these words in *Carols for Today*.

Bible references: Isaiah 9.6, Isaiah 61.1, Jeremiah 23.5, Luke 2.11.

2.

All heaven rings with joyful songs

In the United Kingdom an average of less than 5% attend a place of Christian worship each Sunday. But, at Christmas, nearly one third of the population attend a carol event of some description. The opportunity for sharing the Good News is obvious. When editing *Carols for Today* (published 1986) and *Carol Praise* (published 1987) we had a policy of 'writing back' carols on to folk tunes, so that people who came to church at Christmas only would nevertheless recognize the melody and be able to sing. *All heaven rings* was written in this way to the English folk melody *Barbara Allen*.

Bible reference: Luke 2.13.

3.

All who are thirsty

Music editor David Peacock prepared *World Praise* in the first instance for the 1995 World Baptist Congress in Argentina, for which he had been appointed Music Director. He enlisted me to smooth out some of the horrendous translations of international material that he was receiving. In some cases the results were unconvincing, and, especially where the tune was particularly good, it seemed better to write new English words rather than discard the item altogether. *All who are thirsty* was a case in point: the tune from the Philippines is delightful and should not be lost from the book, but the words we received with it were unusable (and un-revisable!). *Isaiah* 53 inspired a text which lends itself especially to use at the Holy Communion.

Bible reference: Isaiah 55.

4.

Angels, praise him

When I was a boy, I sang in the Anglican choir of Christ Church, Beckenham—south of London, England. I could never fathom why it was necessary to bore people in church—the worst culprit for this was the singing of the canticle '*Benedicite*', mainly during Lent. I promised myself that, when I grew up, I would one day write a version of the *Benedicite* that would be over in two minutes. This version, written when I was about 21, beats the specification by at least thirty seconds. The *Benedicite*, and hence this paraphrase, is based on the *Song of the Three Children* (or *Song of the Three Young Men*—GNB), a short book of the *Apocrypha*. Essentially, it is a hymn of praise for God's blessing in creation.

Bible references: Song of the Three Children verses 29-68. Psalm 22.23, Psalm 22.26, Psalm 33.1, Psalm 64.10, Psalm 69.34, Psalm 107.32, Psalm 135.1, Psalm 148, Psalm 150.

5.
As we walk along beside you/Alleluia, alleluia! As we walk along
In the late 1970's I was just aware of the new renewal song genre that was emerging. This was an attempt at writing a song text, rather than a hymn. There was never a tune in my mind, but it was quickly set to one by Norman Warren ('Burning Heart') in *Hymns for Today's Church*. It probably needs a quiet, meditative tune suitable for use during the administration of Holy Communion. The Alleluia's—or Hallelujah's—are for Easter, and appear in *HTC*—but are in no way necessary.

Bible reference: Luke 24.

6.
Babylon, by the rivers of sorrow
Writing a 'blues' Psalm text to George Gershwin's 'Summertime' was too much of a temptation, and I fell for it. The 'exile' feel is right, as it seems to me. My best memories are of hearing it sung in Nigeria by my friend, the black gospel singer, Geraldine Latty. George Gershwin was out of copyright at the time of writing, but we ran into problems when it was discovered that Ira Gershwin—not out of copyright—had a hand in the melody. Eventually we were given permission to publish.

Bible reference: Psalm 137.

7.
Be gracious to me, Lord
This is an early and simple attempt at a version of Psalm 57 which first appeared in *Psalm Praise*

Bible reference: Psalm 57.

8.
Bethlehem, the chosen city of our God
Written to the Pavane from Peter Warlock's Capriol Suite, this carol has not yet been published to that tune (but to another, by Norman Warren). I have a love-hate relationship with the melody because two boys from the Dulwich College school orchestra had to write an essay on Peter Warlock (Philip Heseltine) as a punishment for misbehaving—I think, playing percussion instruments in a science lesson. One of them grew up to become the Chief Executive of British Telecom, and the other was me. The carol is

meant to evince the lull before the storm, the waiting before the happening of Christmas.

Bible references: Numbers 24.17, Isaiah 11.1, Micah 5.2, Luke 2.8.

9.
Bethlehem, what greater city
The Spanish poet Prudentius (348-c.413) wrote his *Hymnus Epiphaniae*. A selection of stanzas became popular through their insertion in the *Roman Breviary* revised according to the Council of Trent, and published from 1570 onwards. Several English translations are extant, but show signs of aging. It was thought better to retranslate than to revise.

O Sola magnarum urbium
major Bethlem, cui contigit
ducem salutis caelitus
incorporatum gignere:

quem stella, quae solis rotam
vincit decore ac lumine,
venisse terris nuntiat
cum carne terrestri Deum.

videre postquam illum magi,
eoa promunt munera,
stratique votis offerunt
tus, myrram, et aurum regium.

regem Deumque adnuntiant
thesaurus et fragrans odor
turis Sabaei, ac myrreus
pulvis sepulcrum praedocet.

gloria tibi, Domini,
qui apparuisti hodie,
cum Patre et sancto Spiritu
in sempiterna saecula.

Bible references: Micah 5.2, Matthew 2.5.

10.
Blest be the God of Israel/Blessed be the God of Israel
(See: *O bless the God of Israel*)
This was written as *O bless the God of Israel* for *Psalm Praise* and published in that form in 1973. Subsequently it was revised and improved in versions with both first lines. In the United States, Hal H Hopson wrote *Merle's Tune* for this text, and the combination appears in various hymnals.

Approved alternatives now exist as follows:
Stanza 2a
Now from the house of David
a child of grace is given;
a Savior comes among us
to raise us up to heaven . .

Stanza 3b
God guides the feet of pilgrims
along the paths of peace:
O praise our God and Savior,
with songs that never cease!

Bible reference: Luke 1.68.

11.
Blow upon the trumpet
This hymn was written in 1978 in Bitterne, Southampton, at the request of Robin Sheldon, editor of *Songs of Worship*, to employ his tune 'Jonathan'. The tune impressed me with the fanfare-like quality of its first line, hence my choice of the phrase 'Blow upon the trumpet', from the trumpet passages in *Psalm 98, Joel* 2, and *Zechariah* 9. In fact, the hymn was not used by *Songs of Worship* and appeared first in *Hymns for Today's Church*. The *Jubilate Hymns* group suggested a final New Testament stanza. Hence v.4 derives from the trumpet passages in *1 Corinthians* 15 and *1 Thessalonians* 4. There are several tunes available by various *Jubilate* hymns authors, and one by Ken Coates. The use of angular words 'obliterate' and 'mobilizing' are uncharacteristic of my style, but intended to increase the feel of battle, which the trumpet announces.

Bible references: Psalm 98,   Psalm 98.6,   Psalm 98.6,   Isaiah 55.12, Jeremiah 6.1,   Joel 2.1,   Joel 2.1,   Joel 2.1,   Joel 2.15,   Joel 2.31, Zechariah 9.14,   Zechariah 9.14,   Zechariah 9.14,   Matthew 24.31, John 10.1,   Acts 2.20,   1 Corinthians 15.26,   1 Corinthians 15.52, 1 Corinthians 15.57, 1 Thessalonians 4.16, 1 Thessalonians 4.16.

12.
Born as a stranger
A simple carol text addressed directly to Jesus as savior, and written to the tune of Schönster Herr Jesus (*Silesian Folk Songs,* Leipzig 1842).

Bible references: 2 Corinthians 8.9, Hebrews 2.9.

13.
Born of the water
Written in 1980 in Camborne, Cornwall, to meet the need for new baptism hymns. Stanza 1 expresses *Romans* 6 and 8; stanza 2 expounds the joy of fellowship in faith, stanza 3 alludes to 'if a seed fall to the ground and die' (*1 Corinthians* 15) and 'I have called you my friends' (*John* 15); and 'treasures' to the *Ephesians* repeated 'riches of God's grace'. 1.4 'sealed with his promise', relates to Ephesians 2. This has been set to very different tunes, the most remarkable so far by Christopher Norton in *Hymns for the People* (number 33).

Bible references: Psalm 20.4,   Psalm 37.4,   Psalm 87.4,   Isaiah 33.11, Matthew 3.11,   Mark 2.5,   Luke 3.16,   Luke 5.20,   Luke 7.48,   Luke 10.25, John 3.3,   John 3.5,   John 3.5,   John 3.8,   John 3.8,   John 15.15,   Acts 2.38, Acts 3.25,   Romans 5.10,   Romans 6.4,   Romans 6.5,   Romans 6.8, Romans 8.5,   Romans 8.17,   Romans 8.17,   Romans 9.4,   Romans 14.8, Romans 15.2,   2 Corinthians 1.22,   2 Corinthians 1.22,   2 Corinthians 5.18, Galatians 2.19,   Galatians 3.19,   Ephesians 1.5,   Ephesians 1.7,

219

Ephesians 1.13,   Ephesians 1.13,   Ephesians 1.18,   Ephesians 2.7,
Ephesians 3.8,   Ephesians 3.16,   Ephesians 4.30,   Ephesians 4.30,
Philippians 3.10, Colossians 1.22, Philemon 1.6, Hebrews 6.12, James 2.5,
1 Peter 1.3,   1 Peter 3.18,   2 Peter 3.18,   1   John 2.12,   Revelation 1.6,
Revelation 21.7.

14.
Bring to the Lord a glad song
C H H Parry's (1848-1918) tune to Blake's 'And did those feet' is lost to a
wider Christian usage partly because Blake's words are patriotically
English, and partly because they do not constitute a hymn in the sense of
Christian worship. It was with the hope of gaining wider currency both for
the tune and for my words that I decided to write in this meter for *Psalm
Praise* (now see: *Psalms for Today*). This item was first performed in my
hearing by gathered choirs in Manchester cathedral in 1973. It was
subsequently revised for inclusive language, as were so many of the hymns
of the 1950's through to 1980's.

Bible references: 1 Chronicles 15.16,   2 Chronicles 5.12,
2 Chronicles 29.30,   Psalm 96.1,   Psalm 98.1,   Psalm 100,   Psalm 100,
Psalm 149,   Psalm 149,   Psalm 149,   Psalm 150,   Psalm 150,   Isaiah 42.10,
Luke 14.15.

15.
By flowing waters of Babylon
Embarrassingly, the inspiration for this psalm version and its tune came in
the washroom of a caravan site. The site was at the conjunction of
Southampton Water in Hampshire, England, and the stretch of sea between
the Isle of Wight and the mainland, called the Solent. The name of the site,
and hence of the tune, was *Solent Breezes*. It was recorded by the All Souls
Orchestra in its early days, in a vigorous arrangement by Noël Tredinnick.

Bible reference: Psalm 137.

16.
By rivers of sorrow we sat
This is one of several attempts to give *Psalm 137* a usable metrical form.
The Psalm ends vindictively. The problem, for authors who wish to
paraphrase it, is how to be true to the text yet produce a vehicle for
worship. My stanza 3 expresses the destiny of Babylon and Edom as a
warning rather than a threat, and has part of *Psalm 138* as a fitting
conclusion. *Streets of Loredo*, to which this Psalm was written has no
unfortunate associations in the UK. When I tried it out at the North
American Hymn Society plenary in 1989, people were very polite, but some
eyebrows were raised. So, a USA/Canadian tune needed, please!

Bible reference: Psalm 137.

17.
Child in a stable

Dans cette étable
Que Jésus est charmant,
Qu'il est aimable
Dans cet abaissement!
Que d'attraits à la fois!
Tous les palais des rois
N'ont rien de comparable
Aux charmes que je vois
Dans cette étable!

Que sa puissance
Parait bien en ce jour,
Malgré l'enfance
Ou l'a reduit l'amour!
Notre ennemi dompté,
L'enfer déconcerté,
Font voir qu'en sa naissance
Rien n'est si redouté
Que sa puissance.

Child in a stable was the greatest 'translation' challenge I have encountered in my hymn writing. To be true to the original, the last line of each stanza must include a recapitulation of the first. Given this, the rhyme is fairly tight, a difficulty made worse by the fact that some of the lines are so short. Furthermore, the light, end of line, inflections of the French—echoed in the music—do not readily translate into English, especially when they have to rhyme as well!

Bible references: Luke 2.7, Corinthians 1.25.

18.
Child of gladness, child of sorrow
Hymn and song texts which I hesitate to acknowledge get published over the ascription *Word & Music*. This is one that nearly went that way. I am all to conscious of the banality of 'crib today but cross tomorrow'. I hope the rest of the carol is good enough to redeem that one line. If someone can think of an improvement I shall be glad to hear it!

Bible references: Luke 2.34,   Luke 2.34,   2 Corinthians 8.9, 2 Corinthians 8.9.

19.
Child of heaven, born on earth
Il est né le divin enfant,
Jouez haut-bois, resonnez musettes;
Il est né le divin enfant,
Chantons tous son avenement.

Ah! qu'il est beau, qu'il est charmant,
Ah! queses graces sont parfaites!
Ah! qu'il est beau, qu'il est charmant,
Qu'il est doux, ce divin enfant!

Depuis plus de quatre mille ans
Nous le promettaient les prophètes,
Dupuis plus de quatre mille ans
Nous attendions cet heureux temps.

Un étable est son logement,
Un peu de paille sa couchette;
Une etable est son logement,
Pour un Dieu quel a baissement!

Il est né le divin enfant,
Jouez haut-bois, resonnez musettes;
Il est né le divin enfant,
Chantons tous son avenement.

O Jesus, roi tout puissant,
Si petit enfant que vous etes;
O Jesus, roi tout puissant,
Regnez sur nous entièrement.

This was among the French texts I was fed from his base in Brussels by my music editor, David Iliff. I hope I have not taken too many liberties.

Bible references: Luke 2.7, Luke 2.30.

20.
Christ is born to be our king
I cannot remember quite how the carol *Christ is born* came into being, except that it ended up in the hands of David Sanderson who composed the excellent tune that appears to it in *Carol Praise*.

Bible reference: Luke 2.14.

21.
Christ is born within a stable
As a child I attended a 'children's church' in Beckenham, Kent, England—now sucked into the sprawling mass which is Greater London. At Christ Church—to which I owe my call to the ordained ministry—there was a lady who loved to play *Russian Air* on the carillon; in this case a keyboard instrument played in the church tower beneath a huge gray steeple. I always remember Christmas there, in my childhood home town, as a very special season. The bell-like sound of Russian Air made me want to write a carol which would have the bells proclaiming the good news of Jesus' birth. Hence stanza 3 of the carol: "Peal the bells and set them ringing, spread the joyful news abroad."

As far as I remember, this was the first carol specially written for *Carols for Today*, the first of our carol books.

Bible references: Luke 2.7, Luke 2.16.

22.
Christ is king
When *Psalm Praise* was prepared and psalms allotted to each member of the team: Timothy Dudley-Smith, Christopher Idle, Michael Baughen, Richard Bewes, etc., one of my list was Psalm 110—a real teaser. It is obviously a 'royal' psalm; but how do you make it suitable for general worship? Not easily! I failed to get it ready either for *Psalm Praise* or for *Psalms for Today/Songs from the Psalms*. It is improving all the time, but it probably hasn't arrived. I have included it here for completeness, and to remind me to have another try.

Bible reference: Psalm 110.

23.
Christians, make a joyful sound
This carol very loosely based on Latin of c.1500 was made for *Carols for Today* (published 1987).

Resonnet in laudibus   cum jucundis plausibus

Sion cum fide libus:
Apparuit quem genuit Maria!

Christus natus hodie
ex Maria Virgine
sine viruli semine:

Pueri, concinite,
nato Regi psallite,
voce pia dicite:

Sion, lauda Dominum,
salvatorem hominum,
purgatorem criminum:

Deo laus et gloria,
virtus et victoria,
perpete memoria:

(Mainz Cantual, 1605)

Bible references: Luke 2.20, Luke 19.10, John 3.16.

24.
Come and hear the joyful singing
Carols for Today (published 1986) and *Carol Praise* (published 1987) attempted to provide a resource for the very many carol services held before Christmas by churches and schools in the United Kingdom. During this period there is much casual church attendance and it is therefore important to have in the congregational repertoire carols set to familiar tunes. The Welsh traditional tune *Nos Galan* is widely recognized in all parts of the UK as a Christmas melody. But its English associate words are unsuitable for worship:
"Deck the hall with boughs of holly
fa-la-la-la-la, la-la-la-la;
'tis the season to be jolly . . etc."

Hence, if the tune is to be used in this context, different (incarnational) words are needed. *Come and hear the joyful singing* was a fairly artless attempt to provide these. It unashamedly draws on traditional Christmas carol clichés to create an authentic atmosphere and to reflect the traditional melody. It is more *useful* than *poetic*!

Bible references: Isaiah 9.6, Luke 2.11, Luke 2.14, Luke 2.16.

25.
Come and praise the Lord our King
Once again, here is a carol deliberately written onto a folk tune well known in England, thus providing an extra resource for Christmas services when many casual visitors are present. In the carol, the threefold Christmas/Epiphany visitations are celebrated: angels, shepherds, wise men; and we too are encouraged to enter Christ's presence.

Bible references: Matthew 2.11, Luke 2.15.

26.
Come and sing the Christmas story
Again, a widely known melody—even sung by crowds at Welsh rugby football events. Given a good match of words it therefore becomes useful for visitor services, of which there are many in the UK at Christmas-time.

In particular, the custom of Christmas Eve 'midnight' services requires resources. The reference to the angel's announcement and, in particular, the repeated line *this holy night*, make this carol suitable and popular. It is rather more subtle that my others of this genre, moving to a poetic climax in each stanza.

Bible references: Matthew 2.11, Luke 2.1, Luke 2.12, Luke 2.13, Luke 2.13, John 1.14, John 8.12, Philippians 2.7, Philippians 2.7, Colossians 1.27.

27.
Come, join to praise our God
Among contemporary versions of Psalm 89, this text has had to compete with Timothy Dudley-Smith's *Timeless love, we sing the story*, and has usually lost! Ironically, the ending of the hymn is of a style that Timothy—a great encourager of my work in early years—would have recommended.

Bible reference: Psalm 89.

28.
Come, sing praises to the Lord
This was written for *Psalm Praise* (published 1973) in order to capitalize on the popularity in the UK of the *Calypso Carol* melody. It was drafted in simple style for services where there would be children present. Initially, it had the dreadfully awkward (and 'exclusive') second line of the refrain: "Subterranean depths that man defy". Subsequently, when this was replaced for later publications, there were complaints from children and their parents! It appears that had been pleased to discover a long word and resented its loss!

Bible reference: Psalm 95.

29.
Come, worship God who is worthy
A rather more serious attempt to represent *Psalm 95*. This psalm, when used in catholic tradition and Anglican liturgy as the *Venite*, borrows from *Psalm 96* to solve the problem of the otherwise 'negative' ending. In my text, a different device is used to create a fitting conclusion for worship; namely, turning a threat into a joyful consequence—*if* we listen and do not reject God's word to us, we will rejoice. It was first published in 1980 in *Songs of Worship*, Scripture Union.

Bible references: Deuteronomy 32.15, 2 Samuel 22.47, Psalm 18.47, Psalm 24.1, Psalm 89.26, Psalm 95, Psalm 135.5, Ezekiel 34.31, John 10.1, 1 Corinthians 10.26, Hebrews 3.7, Revelation 19.10, Revelation 22.9.

30.
Comes Mary to the grave

Written at Bitterne for the climax of an Easter Sunday evening sermon in 1977, it was first set to music by Norman Warren. At this stage it was offered to *Songs of Worship* (1980) and printed therein. The first time I heard it sung to Norman's tune was at a foretaste of the material in *Hymns for Today's Church* in Westminster Abbey. With its clipped lines it aims to express the simplicity both of the early morning and of the apprehension of Mary Magdalen.

Bible references: Matthew 28.1, Mark 16.1, John 20.1, John 20.11, John 20.16, Acts 2.32, Acts 4.10, Acts 5.30, Acts 10.40, Acts 13.37, Romans 10.9, 1 Corinthians 6.14, Galatians 1.1, Ephesians 2.6, Colossians 2.12, 1 Peter 1.21.

31.
Commit your way to God the Lord
"Commit your life to the Lord, trust in him and he will act," says the psalm (*New English Bible* version). Here is a simple, short and usable, if not specially adequate, version of a somewhat long original. The last stanza picks up on the phrasing of the first and draws all to a conclusion.

Bible reference: Psalm 37.

32.
Creator of the stars of light
This Latin text of which *Creator of the stars of light* is a translation, was in general use as an evening hymn of the Latin rite (apart from the Ambrosian and Mozarabic): it is found in the Canterbury Hymnal of the tenth century. The *Hymns Ancient & Modern* commentary observes, "It is anonymous, but probably belongs to the early middle ages, when scansion by accent was superseding scansion by quality."

Conditor alme siderum,
aeterna lux credentium,
Christe, redemptor omnium,
exaudi preces supplicum:

qui, condolens interitu
mortis perire saeculum,
salvasti mundum languidum,
donans reis remedium:

vergente mundi vespere,
uti sponsus de thalamo,
egressus honestissima
virginis matris clausula.

Occasum Sol custodiens,
Luna pallorem retinens,
candor in astra reluccens

castos observans limites.

cujus forti potentiae
genu curvantur omnia;
caelestia, terrestria
fatentur mutu subdita.

te deprecamur, hagie,
venture judex saeculi,
conserva nos in tempore
hostis a telo perfidi.

laus, honor, virtus, gloria
Deo Patri cum Filio
sancto simul Paraclito
in sempiterna saecula.

The tune *Conditor Alme* is that most chiefly associated with these words, and therefore with J M Neale's translation, *Creator of the starry height*, but other Long Meter tunes, such as *Veni Creator* will do. The new text was written as part of the Advent seasonal provision in *Carols for Today* (Hodder & Stoughton 1986). For a shorter version, omit my stanzas 4 and 5.

Bible references: Luke 1.31,   Luke 1.42,   Luke 2.5,   Romans 4.25, Romans 6.4, Romans 6.13, Colossians 1.16, Hebrews 1.2.

33.
Down from the height
Philippians 2.6-11 is widely recognized as one of the earliest Christian hymns. It is therefore an invitation and a challenge to any hymn writer. This paraphrase was written in conjunction with my book *I Paul*, which tells Paul's adventurous story in the first person. The hymn was put into the mouths of Paul and Silas when at midnight in the Philippian jail they were heard 'singing praises to God' (*Acts* 16.25).

The rhyme here is A, B, B, A—but the 'near' rhyme between the 'A' and the 'B' lines has proved a little too close for comfort! At least the hymn keeps to the text!

Bible reference: Philippians 2

34.
Fear not, for I bring all people good
At David Peacock's suggestion I wrote these words to the public domain melody made popular by the chorus *Come into his presence singing, 'Alleluia'*. It was first published in *Carol Praise* (1987). The tune is there set as a round, again adding interest to a collection of music for Christmas worship. The text is entirely based on the *Luke* 2 announcement by the angels of the birth of Jesus.

Bible reference: Luke 2.10.

35.
Fling wide the gates
Based on *Psalm 24*, this hymn was created to utilize the tune *Crucifer* by Sydney Nicholson (1875-1947). It first appeared in *Church Family Worship* (published 1986). In 1990 it was used at the *Jubilate* launch of *Psalms for Today* at London's *Royal Albert Hall*. Taking part were many of *Jubilate*'s friends and associates, including actor David Suchet. *The All Souls Orchestra & Choir* were joined by the massed choirs of the *Royal School of Church Music*, for whom *Crucifer* has important significance; hence its use on this occasion.

Bible reference: Psalm 24

36.
Food to pilgrims given

Written for *World Praise* as an English language text to parallel the Korean but not, in this case a paraphrase or translation. The references are obviously eucharistic—but have resonances with the wilderness experience of 'mana'

Bible references: Genesis 14.18, Exodus 16, Leviticus 21.22, Numbers 11, Nehemiah 19.5, Daniel 9.4, Matthew 6.10, Matthew 26.26, Matthew 26.42, Mark 14.22, Luke 11.2, Luke 22.19, Luke 24.30, John 6, John 7.38, 1 Corinthians 11.24.

37.
From heaven above I come to bring
The translation follows Martin Luther (1483-1546).

'Vom Himmel hoch,
da komm ich her,
ich bring' euch gute neue Mär,
der guten Märbring ich so viel,
davon ich singen und sagen will.

'Euch ist ein Kindlein heut' gebor'n
von einer JungFrau, auserkor'n;
ein Kindelein so zart und lein,
das soll eu'r Freud' und Wonne sein.

'Es ist der Herr Christ unser Gott,
der will euch führ'n aus aller Not,
er will eu'r Heiland selber sein,
von allen Sünden machen rein.

'Er bringt euch alle Seligkeit,
die Gott, der Vater, hat bereit',
dass ihr mit uns im Himmelreich
sollt leben nun und ewiglich.

'So merket nun das Zeichen recht,

die Krippen, Windelein so schlecht:
Da findet ihr das Kind gelegt,
das alle Welt erhält und trägt.'

Des lasst uns alle fröhlich sein
und mit den Hirten geh'n hinein,
zu seh'n, was Gott uns hat beschert,
mit seinem lieben Sohn verehrt.

Merk auf, mein Herz, und sieh dort hin:
Was liegt doch in dem Krippelein?
Was ist das schöne Kindelein?
Es ist das liebe Jesulein.

Sei uns willkomm'n, du edler Gast!
Den Sünder nicht verschmähet hast
und kommst ins Elend her zu mir,
wie soll ich immer danken dir?

Martin Luther (1483-1546)

The translation was first published in *Carol Praise* (HarperCollins, 1987)

Bible reference: Luke 2.9.

38.
From highest heaven where praises ring
See: *From heaven above I come to bring*
This form of the text was prepared for *Carols for Today*, for the tune *Echo Carol*.

Bible references: Luke 2.7, 2 Corinthians 8.9, Philippians 2.7.

39.
From time beyond my memory
The *Psalm 71* paraphrase was prepared for *Psalms for Today* (published 1990). The tune *Passons* was written by American pastor Keith Landis, whose address in California contains the word 'Passons'. Keith had that

most dreaded experience of seeing the house burn where he kept all his manuscripts; he was, however, able to extract the most important material before his study ignited.

"You are my hope, O Lord . . . my protector since my mother's womb," exclaims the psalmist. My text tries to convey the sense of faith through time; past, present and future.

Bible reference: Psalm 71.

40.
Gabriel the angel came
There is reference in Chaucer (*The Miller's Tale*) to this mediaeval carol. Nicholas the 'Clerk of Oxenford' sang it in the evening to the accompaniment of his 'gay sautrye' . . .

'On which he made a nighte's melodye
so swetely that al the chambre rong,
and *Angelus ad Virginem* he song.'

Angelus ad Virginem
subintrans in conclave
Virginis formidinem
demulcens, inquit, 'Ave!
ave regina virginum;
coeli terraeque Dominum
   concipies
   et paries
   intacta
salutem hominum;
tu porta coeli facta,
medela criminum.'

'Quomodo conciperem
quae virum non cognovi?
Qualiter infringerem
quod firma mente vovi?'
'Spiritus Sancti gratia
perficiet haec omnia;
   ne timeas,
   sed gaudeas,
   secura
quod castimonia
manebit in te pura
Dei potentia.'

Ad haec virgo nobilis
respondens inquit ei:
'Ancilla sum humilis
omnipotentis Dei.
Tibi coelesti nuntio,
tanti secreti conscio,
   onsentiens,
   et cupiens
   videre
factum quod audio;
parata sum parere,
Dei consilio.'

Eia mater Domini,
quae pacem reddidisti
angelis et homini,
cum Christum genuisti;
tuum exora filium
ut se nobis propitium
   exhibeat,
   et deleat
   peccata:
praestans auxilium
vita frui beata
post hoc exsilium.

Bible reference: Luke 1.26.

41.
Give thanks to God, for he is good
This was first written as a *spoken* responsive psalm for the service book *Church Family Worship* (published 1986). Hence the lack of any rhyme,

which I would usually work towards. The traditional Hebrew response *His love shall last for ever* was to be repeated by the congregation after every line by the minister. Despite the fact that it was to be spoken, it was devised in meter to keep the psalm moving along. Only afterwards did I realize that it could be sung to a standard 8887 tune, of which *I saw three ships* is a folk example and suitable for use in a congregation with children present.

Bible reference: Psalm 136.

42.
Given by grace
During my first years as Vicar of Tonbridge it was impressed upon me how gracious was the Lord's provision of the Holy Communion; I saw people being blessed as we prayed for them during the reception of the bread and wine. This text was written in response to that experience. I confess again to Timothy Dudley-Smith's influence in my stanza 3, line 2—'who loved and came'. Timothy's *Had he not loved us,* in which this is the concluding line, is in my opinion his very finest work. I recall telling him of my admiration for it when we were discussing which of our texts we felt most satisfied with. At the time we were jay-walking into Trafalgar Square; he had no fear of traffic!

Bible references: Matthew 26.26,   Mark 14.22,   Luke 22.19, 1 Corinthians 11.24.

43.
Glad music fills the Christmas sky
This was one out of due time; it was written for *Hymns for Today's Church* and before the idea for the carol books struck me. Unusually for me, it did not emerge from a chosen Bible text, but was more a gentle musing on the contrast of sensations: the praise of the angels, and ours, and the tender emotion of Mary—concluding that both celebration and contemplation must contribute to our worship of the Christ child.

Bible references: 2 Chronicles 29.30,   2 Chronicles 29.30,   Luke 1.46, Luke 1.46,   Luke 2.13,   Luke 2.13,   Luke 2.13,   Luke 2.13,   Luke 2.14, Luke 2.14,   Luke 2.16,   Luke 2.16,   Luke 2.19,   Luke 2.19,   Luke 2.19, 1 Peter 1.12, 1 Peter 1.12.

44.
Glory and honor
This was a late contribution to *Psalms for Today.* It is not, of course, a psalm, but a representation of the Anglican canticle *Glory and honor* from the *Alternative Service Book 1980,* based on *Revelation* 4 and 5. I remember being asked to lead worship using my material at the Westminster Choir College, Princeton summer school of 1989. Ironically for me as the only English person present (or by some fiendish plot), it was

American Independence Day. I do remember that we sung this text to *Schönster Herr Jesu.*

Bible references: Revelation 4.11, Revelation 5.9.

45.
Glory be to God in heaven
In 1979/80 when we were preparing *Hymns for Today's Church,* there was felt to be a need for a new version of the historic *Gloria*—the 4th century Greek hymn of which the opening sentence is taken from *Luke* 2.14. *Glory be to God in heaven* was written in 1981 in the Lake District in response to that call. The 'Gloria' is preserved in Church of England use in both 1662 and 1980 communion rites, and likewise in the liturgy of the United Church of Canada and the Reformed Church of America etc. I probably wrote it to *Abbot's Leigh,* but it is usually set to Beethoven's *Ode to Joy.* One of the characteristics of the *Gloria* is its internal compromise between celebration and penitence. This dual personality makes it very difficult to order liturgically. The penitence is represented here by the to the second stanza; the celebration is in the shape of the stanzas, making it suitable for use with vigorous tunes.

The most celebrated use of *Glory be to God in heaven* was for a vast open-air Papal Mass in Melbourne, Australia on August 1st 1986

Bible references: Mark 16.19,   Luke 2.13,   Luke 19.38,   John 1.18, John 1.29, Philippians 2.11.

46.
Glory in the highest heaven
John Barnard composed the tune *Guiting Power* (a village in the English Cotswold hills) for Michael Saward's *Christ triumphant, ever reigning.* This was the tune in my mind when *Glory in the highest heaven* was written. John was, quite reasonably, unhappy about using his tune to anything other than *Christ triumphant* while it was becoming established—at least, that is how he graciously explained the case to me! *Glory in the highest heaven* was therefore first published to *Angel voices.* In order to switch between tunes I had to make some adjustments of emphasis, but it still works to both. I greatly admire the construction of *Angel voices ever singing,* and endeavor to reflect the internal rhyming which Francis Pott achieves in that hymn.

Bible references: Matthew 2.1, Luke 2.14.

47.
Glory to the Lord of love
David Peacock, when compiling the second half of *World Praise* in readiness for the 1995 World Baptist Congress in Argentina, drew my attention to this tune. It is by Henry Kiley, and reflects a Kalinga melody.

He calls it *Mary's Salidumay*. David asked me if I would write an English *Magnificat* which might be sung to this tune. Hence *Glory to the Lord of love.*

Bible references: Genesis 17.4, 1 Samuel 2.1, Psalm 86.5, Psalm 86.15, Luke 1.46, John 14.6

48.
God is king—be warned, you mighty
It was the case with both *Jubilate* Psalm projects (*Psalm Praise*, 1973; *Psalms for Today/Songs from the Psalms*, 1990) that we divided up the *Psalter* among a group of hymn-writers. For *Psalm Praise*, this was done mathematically! Some of the great Timothy Dudley Smith and Christopher Idle hymns can be attributed to this procedure. Only when one of us failed to produce a worthy version were the others let loose on our patch! By the time I came to edit *Psalms for Today/Songs from the Psalms*, there were many more contemporary psalm versions available—but usually the easy ones. In other words, writers had naturally gone for the psalms which were already suitable for general worship. Once again we distributed psalm numbers among competent writers. Among those who responded this time were: Adrian Cleaton, Basil Bridge, Timothy Dudley-Smith, Brian Foley, Stephen Horsfall, Christopher Idle, Graham Kendrick, Molly Knight, Keith Landis, David Mowbray, David Preston, Paul Wigmore, Stephen Wilcockson, Barbara Woollett—many of them making substantial contributions. Even so, there remained a body of 'difficult' psalms, of which this was one. So, as editor, I felt I had to tackle them myself. I was fortunate in having editorial colleagues who could be devastatingly critical—and were! Hence not all my work escaped into the books. I well remember being hauled up to the House of Lords by our *Jubilate* Chairman, Bishop Michael Baughen, to be questioned as to why so many of these psalm versions were by me. I replied that nobody else wanted to do them!

God is king—be warned, you mighty transposes a fairly judgmental psalm into an encouragement to righteousness and to Godliness for both land and leadership.

Bible reference: Psalm 82.

49.
50.
God is our fortress and our rock
One of the first pieces written at Eversley when, in 1981, I assumed the pastoral mantle of Charles Kingsley, also once Rector of the parish. I received translation help for this paraphrase from a visit by Annemarie Von Rad, daughter-in-law of the world-famous Old Testament theologian Gerhard Von Rad, and herself a considerable English scholar. The three main previous English translations are:

'A safe stronghold our God is still' by Thomas Carlyle,
'A mighty fortress' by Frederick Henry Hedge and others, and
'A mighty stronghold is our God' by Honor Mary Thwaites.

All have become considerably archaic now. I have inevitably reflected them to some extent because of the constraints of the meter of *Ein' Feste Burg*, and of the original text. I hope I have done justice to Martin Luther; my only regret is that I was forced to omit Luther's line from the psalm 'a little word shall slay him' (ein wortlein).

Ein' feste Burg ist unser Gott,	Und wenn die Welt voll Teufel war'
Ein' gute Wehr und Waffen.	Und woilt' uns gar verschlingen,
Er hilft uns frei aus aller Not	So furchten wir uns nicht zu sehr,
Die uns jetzt has betroffen.	Es soll uns doch gelingen,
Der alte bose Feind	Der Furst von dieser Welt
Mit Ernst er es jetzt meint;	Wie sauer er sich steilt,
Gross' Macht und viele List	So tut er uns doch nicht;
Sein' grausam' Rustung ist;	Das macht, er ist gericht't,
Auf Erd'n ist nicht sein's Gleichen.	Ein Wortlein kann ihn fallen.
Mit uns'rer Macht ist nichts getan,	Das Wort sie sollen lassen stah'n
Wir sind gar bald verloren;	Und kein'n Dank dazu haben;
Es streit't fur uns der rechte Mann,	Er ist bei uns wohl auf dem Plan
Den Gott hat selbst erkoren.	Mit seinem Geist und Gaben.
Und fragst du Wer der ist?	Nehmen sie uns den Leib,
Er heisset Jesus Christ,	Gut, Ehre, Kind und Weib;
Der Herre Zebaoth;	Lass fahren nur dahin,
Und ist kein and'rer Gott;	Sie haben's kein'n Gewinn;
Das Feld muss er behalten.	Das Reich muss uns doch bleiben.

As regards the meter of this hymn, traditions vary. The so-called 'rhythmic' form is not found to any degree in the UK. Both are found in the USA. A fascinating Concertato by Ed Nowak, using this text in parallel with one from the *Lutheran Book of Worship* (nearly identical to that in *Worship II*), and one by Dennis Newman, was published by *G.I.A.* (Chicago) in 1988.

Bible references: Deuteronomy 32.4, 2 Samuel 22.2, 2 Samuel 22.3, Esther 3.8, Psalm 18.2, Psalm 18.2, Psalm 18.31, Psalm 31.2, Psalm 46.1, Psalm 59.16, Psalm 62.2, Psalm 71.3, Psalm 78.35, Psalm 83.2, Psalm 91.2, Psalm 115.9, Psalm 144.2, Isaiah 44.8, Isaiah 94.22, Jeremiah 16.19, Habakkuk 3.17, Matthew 6.13, Luke 11.4, John 12.31, John 12.31, John 14.30, John 14.30, John 16.11, John 16.11, Acts 6.7, Acts 12.24, Titus 2.13, Hebrews 4.12, Hebrews 12.28, 1 Peter 1.13, 1 Peter 3.15, Revelation 6.2, Revelation 19.11.

51.

God is with the righteous

I remember going to an open air concert at Kenwood (similar, I suppose, to the Hollywood Bowl, or Ravinia near Chicago). For some reason or other, the orchestra played as a light number an arrangement of a traditional

American melody made internationally popular because of civil rights movements in the 1950's, *We shall not be moved*. It occurred to me that this sentiment accorded with that of *Psalm 1*, '. . he is like a tree planted by streams of water'. We were in need of a lighter version of *Psalm 1* for *Songs from the Psalms*—hence this text.

Bible reference: Psalm 1.

52.
God of light and life's creation
Written in 1976 at Bitterne for 'Consecration Sunday', a local invention. This was the Sunday most conveniently near the anniversary of the consecration of the Church, a day on which the ministers and all the lay workers dedicated themselves to God's service in the coming year. It is a hymn based on Solomon's prayer of dedication (*2 Chronicles* 6), designed for the celebration of the consecration or dedication of a place of worship. There was an extra stanza ('God of promise, God of honor . . hear your people in their pain, turn towards this house again') which spoke of the threat of war; this was omitted in *Hymns for Today's Church* and subsequently lost. The hymn was written to the tune 'All Saints'. I asked for this hymn to be used at my induction as Rector of Eversley.

Bible references: Genesis 1.3, 1 Kings 8.23, 2 Chronicles 6.14, Luke 2.12, John 4.20, Romans 14.8.

53.
God our Father, bless your people/God our Shepherd, bless your people
Written in 1979 at Bitterne (as 'God our *Father*, bless . .), to meet the need for hymns on a unity theme. The 'communion', union', 'dominion', 'Three in One' rhyme is somewhat ambitious; David Iliff and Paul Edwards have nobly tried to cope with it in their tunes.

The "Shepherd" variant is to provide for use where language needs to be inclusive in the 'God' sense.

Bible references [Psalm 28.9, Psalm 80.1, Micah 7.14,] Jeremiah 32.39, Jeremiah 32.39, Jeremiah 32.39, Matthew 26.26, Matthew 26.26, Matthew 26.26, John 17.11, John 17.11, John 17.11, Acts 4.32, Acts 4.32, Acts 4.32.

54.
God save and bless our nation
This hymn and its unpublished tune (called 'Bramshill') were written in the English Lake District in 1981 in honor of the Police Staff College at Bramshill in Hampshire, where I served as chaplain and lecturer in Christian ethics etc. from 1981—1987. Though never used in that context, the words were published in *Hymns for Today's Church*. There had been a

call from the *Jubilate* team for a national hymn which was neither pompous nor triumphalist.

Bible references: Matthew 4.1, Luke 24.15.

55.

God speaks—the Lord of all the earth
'The Mighty One, God the Lord, speaks . .' So begins *Psalm 50*; and continues 'Hear, my people and I will speak'. God, as the great judge, summons the earth, so that he may correct the false understanding that God is swayed by sacrifice when there is no thankfulness. Neither will God accept worship from the wicked. Sacrifice from a thankful heart simply prepares the way for God to show his saving grace. This Psalm version was completed for my *Psalms for Today* (1990)

Bible reference: Psalm 50.

56.

God the Father caused to be
One of three credal forms (see also: *God the Father of creation* and *I believe in God the Father*) written in Bitterne, Southampton in approximately 1977 to meet a need for musical 'Affirmations of faith' at guest services. Of the three, this was not ready for *Hymns for Today's Church* (published 1981). It was, however complete for the publication of *Church Family Worship* in 1986, where an affirmation of faith was needed for each chapter. Stanza 1, line 3 is the only remarkable line; emphasizing a renaissance in the churches in those years—art and life were to be re-affirmed as renewal swept across Christendom.

Bible references: John 1.1, John 1.32.

57.

God the Father of creation
Written in approximately 1977. One of three credal forms (see also: *God the Father caused to be* and *I believe in God the Father*) written in Bitterne, Southampton to meet a need for musical 'Affirmations of faith' at guest services. The plural 'We believe . . .' reflects the plural form of creed, first introduced into the Church of England in the 'Series 3' communion rite, and then preserved in *Rite A* of the *Alternative Service Book 1980*. Stanza 3 again reflects my fascination with *Romans* 8. Stanza 1, line 3 echoes Solomon's prayer of dedication in the temple. Stanza 4, line 2 asserts the Trinity as a heavenly reality to which we respond.

Bible references: Psalm 119.25, Psalm 125.1, Romans 8.26.

58.

God whose love we cannot measure
This hymn is based upon the prayer which follows, attributed to St. Boniface (680—754):

234

O God, whose love we cannot measure,
nor ever number your blessings:
we thank you that
   in our darkness you are our light,
   in our weakness you are our strength,
   in our sorrows comfort and peace;
and from everlasting to everlasting,
you are our God,
Father, Son and Holy Spirit. **Amen.**

The hymn has not yet been published in the UK, but has appeared in at least one American book, to the tune *Silver Creek* by Roy Hopp (Selah Publishing Co. Inc.). The hymn tries to mirror the prayer and not to add too much in the process; the final lines of the hymn pick up the theme of the first line and move to a conclusion.

Bible references: Exodus 6.7, Leviticus 26.12, Isaiah 9.2, Ezekiel 36.28, Micah 7.8, Luke 1.79, John 1.5, John 12.46, Acts 26.18, 2 Corinthians 4.6, Ephesians 3.19, Ephesians 5.8.

59.
God will arise because the weak
"For the ruin of the poor, for the groans of the needy, now I will arise," says the Lord. This psalm version, designed for *Songs from the Psalms* (published 1990) was deliberately styled as a song, and not fixed to any traditional meter. Here I seized upon the graphic qualities of the psalm for impact and life. As a result it is 'very psalmy' and most sensibly used in a liturgical psalm context.

Bible reference: Psalm 12.

60.
Happiness is simple trust
Something I have never done before or since—I decided to enter a hymn competition in the late nineteen-eighties. It was run by a television company; I believe the twin themes for which hymns might be written were *The Beatitudes* or *Holy Communion*.

I decided to write from the *Matthew* 5 text—as simply as possible, expressing what I believed lay behind the sentiments of this marvelous rabbinic-style lesson of Jesus. For instance, the 'mourning' in 'Blessed are those who mourn' is not fundamentally or primarily about people who, however sadly, suffer human bereavement, but about those who are in mourning for the absence of Godly standards and truth. Just as hunger in the *Beatitudes* is not, of course, purely about stomach pains! The other problem for present-day translators of the *Beatitudes* is that the word 'blessed' as traditionally pronounced ("bless-ed") has lost all its connotation of God's blessing; the only surviving uses of bless-ed are in the description "bless-ed nuisance", or as a slang term meaning ultra-pietistic (as in "he is rather bless-ed, isn't he?"). *Today's English Version* (*Good News Bible*) employs 'happy': "Happy are those who . ." But 'happy' seems trivial for the task; it does not convey either enough depth, or enough divinity. My way was to use the 'happy' root, but to let the text define its meaning.

I sent the text to a *Jubilate* musician (who shall be nameless!) for a tune, assuming he would send it on to the competition. He forgot! But I am glad to say that Fred Kaan won with his incomparable *Put peace into each other's hands*—a valuable asset to any hymnal.

Bible references: Matthew 5.3, Luke 6.20.

61.
Happy Christmas, everybody

This is quite awful—isn't it? Well I suppose a better tune than mine could redeem it. I put it in as a marker. Back in the 1960's, the way Anglican churches were chanting canticles was really bad, and boring for a new generation. Out of sympathy for them I attempted a song-style rewriting of the Anglican canticles at Morning and Evening Prayer. When I discovered that Michael Baughen had a similar project in mind (eventually to become *Psalm Praise*), I half jokingly proposed a form of the canticle *Jubilate* which began "Jubilate everybody . . .", and a form of the canticle *Nunc Dimittis* which began "O let me go . . "! Michael never took me up on the *Nunc Dimittis* but, to my surprise, his team went for my "Jubilate everybody"! A few years after its publication in *Psalm Praise*, another text beginning "Jubilate everybody" emerged from another writer and another publisher. Timothy Dudley-Smith wrote to me that I should protest and take action. I did in fact inform the publisher about the plagiarized text, but I hadn't the heart to do more because Fred Dunn's version was much better than mine!

When David Peacock and I were looking for more carol texts for *Carol Praise* (published 1987) I obliged with this Christmas carol to my old 'Jubilate everybody' tune. It won't fit the Fred Dunn melody!

Bible references: Isaiah 42.6, Isaiah 49.6, Isaiah 60.3, Luke 2.32.

62.
He lives in us, the Christ of God

Written in 1977 in Bitterne, as a consequence of an early translation of this chapter of the *Epistle to the Romans*. (My translation later passed to a more thorough work published by Creative Publishing, 1983). The hymn was included in *Songs of Worship* (published 1980). Stanza 1 reflects Paul's experience. Stanza 2 reflects real personal and continuing pastoral experience. Stanza 3 is the great assurance of St. Paul about the inalienable love of God.

He lives in us later met up with an outstanding melody, *Rachel*, by Chris Bowater, appearing to an arrangement by Noël Tredinnick in the *Jubilate/HarperCollins* publication, *Come, Rejoice!* (1989).

Bible references: Isaiah 50.8, Romans 8, Romans 8, 1 John 4.13.

63. Heal me, hands of Christ
64. Heal me, hands of Jesus

This hymn was written at Bitterne in 1981. The *Jubilate* team realized that there was a shortage of hymns about healing. The hymn reflects a pastoral concern for the mentally ill and those who have burdens of anxiety which they cannot share. Words and phrases like 'restore my hope', 'bitterness', 'memories of guilt', are deliberately planted; as is the concept of forgiveness removing bitterness and bringing peace.

The hymn was originally written as 'Heal me, hands of Christ'. Norman Warren, when composing the tune *Sutton Common* to this hymn (for *Hymns for Today's Church*) asked for an alternative opening line 'Heal me, hands of Jesus', on the grounds that it was an altogether gentler opening for a hymn about Jesus, and better reflected the Gospel narratives of Jesus healing. I agreed, and made the consequent change to the text—especially to the last line, 'for Jesus brings me peace'. Both texts are now available but, as far as I am aware only the 'Jesus' text is in print (USA and UK).

Bible references: Matthew 6.12,   Matthew 8.3,   Matthew 17.7, Matthew 18.21,   Matthew 19.3,   Mark 1.41,   Mark 5.27,   Mark 8.23, Mark 11.25,   Luke 4.40,   Luke 5.13,   Luke 11.4,   Luke 22.51, Ephesians 4.32,   Philippians 4.7,   Colossians 3.13,   Colossians 3.15, Hebrews 9.14, Hebrews 9.22, Hebrews 10.22, 1 John 1.7, 1 John 3.19.

65.

Hear me, O Lord, and respond to my prayer
'Turn to me, Lord, and answer . . guard me. . among the gods not one is like you . . guide me in your truth . . let me walk in your way . . fill your servant's heart with joy . . give me proof of your kindness.' These are the sentiments that informed my *Psalm 86* paraphrase, initially for *Psalms for Today*. Composers Gareth Green and Derek Williams responded with the tunes that may be found in that book.

Bible reference: Psalm 86.

66.

Hear the skies around
During the process leading up to the compilation of *Carols for Today*, we alerted friends in Europe who might be able to discover carols from that continent which had attractive tunes, but had no English translation (or no adequate translation for purposes of contemporary worship). Among texts

that arrived at my home was the English translation of a Yugoslavian carol *Rajske strune zadonite*. I cannot now remember whether *Hear the skies around* truly matched the original, or whether I decided to begin from *Luke 2.8 ff*. We certainly used the tune, however.

Bible reference: Luke 2.14.

67.
Here we come a-caroling
Certainly not a profound text! But another attempt to bring a folk carol into worship potential. The original text to this traditional north of England folk melody begins 'Here we come a-wassailing among the leaves so green'—words from Husk's *Songs of the Nativity* (1896) *Jubilate* music editor, David Iliff challenged me to write a contemporary text in the run up to a future revision of *Carol Praise* for *HarperCollins*. Since David does not really approve of this attempt, I have included it for completeness, not with pride!

Bible references: Luke 2.7, Luke 2.8.

68.
How blessed are those who trust in God/How blessed are those who live by faith
A set of Old Testament beatitudes: what an interesting discovery—for me, at least. We are all conscious of the 'beatitude' of *Psalm 1*, 'Blessed is the man . . 'But I had not realized that this was here in *Psalm 112*. 'Happy is the man who fears the Lord . .'' In order to preserve the inclusive sense I set the psalm in the plural. And I emphasized the 'beatitude' idea by repeating "How blessed . .", "How happy . .", etc. at the outset of each stanza. The close meter appealed to me for simple statements; this involved some fairly tight expressions, using poetic devices, as stanza 2, line 2:

"who justly deal and kindly care"

and two sets of half rhymes (in alternate stanzas):

"care"/"here", "given"/"heaven".

The doxology may be of interest. It is often easy to leave a doxology with a three person God, unresolved into a Unity. Here, in stanza four, the three person nature of the Godhead is stated first, then unified in the final lines as one God who has functions that are obviously those of Father ("loved us"), Son ("came to save") and Spirit ("fills our hearts with grace from heaven").

Either first line is available: in some ways I prefer ". . trust in God" for its simplicity. ". . live by faith" avoids the repeated "God", but has 'faith mission' connotations; a cliché not intended here. I suggest either:

"How blessed/blest are those who ***trust in God,***
delighting in ***his*** sure command."

or:

"How blessed/blest are those who *live by faith,*
delighting in *God's* sure command."

Bible reference: Psalm 112.

69.

How shall they hear the word of God
This is a hymn for communicators, commissioned in the late 1970's by 'BBC Radio Solent' to mark their tenth anniversary, and for use in their celebration service broadcast from Winchester Cathedral. The words have been published more widely in the USA than in the UK.

Based on *Romans* 10, the hymn is dedicated to "those who speak where many listen". There much to be done and many in need of God. The hymn concludes with a commitment to proclaim the Good News of Jesus Christ by actions as well as by words.

Bible references: Isaiah 6.8, Matthew 9.38, Matthew 24.14, Mark 13.10, John 17.18, John 20.21, Romans 10.14.

70.

Hush, little baby; peace, little boy
Yet another attempt to utilize a folk tune for the demands of worship services during busy Christmases in the UK. This was prepared for, and published in *Carol Praise* (1987). Here again I should probably be hiding behind my pseudonym *Word & Music* as it is modest poetry. Chris Idle, asked for his response to the draft, replied, "Oh no! Not *more* hay." But someone may find it useful because the tune is so easy and so well known.

Bible reference: Luke 2.5.

71.

I believe in God the Father
One of three credal forms (see also: *God the Father caused to be* and *God the Father of creation*) written at Bitterne, Southampton in approximately 1997 to meet a need for musical 'affirmations of faith' at guest services. Here God the Father is portrayed as creator and sustainer, God the Son as redeemer and conqueror of death, and the Holy Spirit as energizer, and mark of our divine ownership.

Bible references: Genesis 1.1, Genesis 1.1, Genesis 2.4, Psalm 19.14, Isaiah 33.11, Isaiah 41.14, Isaiah 42.5, Matthew 3.11, Matthew 27.35, Matthew 28.19, Mark 15.24, Luke 3.16, Luke 23.33, John 3.8, John 19.18, Acts 2.1, Acts 2.26, Romans 1.20, Romans 6.6, 1 Corinthians 2.2, 2 Corinthians 1.22, Galatians 3.14, Galatians 4.6, Ephesians 1.13, Ephesians 4.30, Colossians 1.16, 1 Thessalonians 5.19, 1 Timothy 4.4, Hebrews 1.2, Revelation 1.18, Revelation 4.11.

72.
I cried out for heaven to hear me
"I cried aloud to God and he heard me . . In my distress I sought the Lord .
. I remembered forgotten years . . O Lord, I recall your wonders in times
gone by . . the clouds poured water, the skies thundered . . you guided your
people like a flock of sheep." *Psalm 77* recalls the despair of the fleeing
people of Israel and the miracle of the Red Sea deliverance. It encourages
the people of God to trust their Savior, despite what seems to be. This is a
true psalm of comfort. It was prepared for, and first published in *Psalms
for Today* (1990).

Bible reference: Psalm 77.

I have no strength but yours (see: I will give thanks to the Lord most
high)

73.
I love you, Lord, my rock
Psalm 18 is surely one of the most powerful psalms of personal devotion.
When I was editing *Psalms for Today* there was no shortage of writers
wanting to set this one. It is startling with its combination of graphic—even
violent—imagery, and love song. Originally, my text moved between
second and third person references to God, as does the psalm—"you",
"he", "you", "he" etc. However, because of inclusive language sensibilities
in the USA I have kept the text here to "you" (second person singular).

Bible reference: Psalm 18.

74.
I praise you, Lord, with all my heart
Here is a psalm of judgment—justice for a wicked world in which the
faithful singer is trapped. It promises: justice will be done. In phrasing it
for worship, I have simply let the psalm affirm God's justice, the ultimate
folly of wickedness and the certitude of God's faithfulness.

Bible reference: Psalm 9.

75.
I will give thanks to the Lord most high
This text was prepared in song style for *Song from the Psalms* (published
1990). It was set to music by Chris Rolinson as *I have no strength but
yours*, with two lines added to the refrain, and omitting its first occurrence.

Here again is a psalm that was difficult to paraphrase for worship because
of the sentiments expressed—so it was left to the Editor! Rather than
employ the vindictiveness of many 'difficult' psalm texts I tended to opt for
the divine justice 'principle' which should rightly take the place of a cry for
revenge. i.e. I would translate the idea "Lord, crush the wicked", say, with
the idea "People will be crushed if they are wicked". *Psalm 7* is a pointer

in this regard. Although God is told, "Rouse yourself in wrath against my foes," the psalmist assents that the wicked person's "mischief shall recoil upon himself, his violence shall fall on his own head". And that applies to me too! "Lord, if I have done any of these things, trample my life to the ground and lay my honor in the dust."

All in all, this is a psalm true to life, and true to human nature, and I am glad that I had the opportunity to paraphrase it, for there is much encouragement here. We must put any bitterness into the hands of God, and allow him to redeem it through our praise.

Bible reference: Psalm 7.

76.
If we love the word of God/If you love the word of God
How do you render *Psalm 1* without being offensive to the increasing number of people who are conscious and/or sensitive to 'exclusive' (gender) language? Obviously, you can set it in the plural:
"Blessed are those who . . delight in the law of the Lord",
and I believe this is a perfectly proper procedure for a hymn-writer.

Another way, however, is to put the whole text in conditional language; for example:
"If you . . delight in the law of the Lord, you will be blessed."
Or:
"If we . . delight in the law of the Lord, we will be blessed".

Here I offer both options; including the more bland, "If we love . . etc." because I am not sure if the apparently more aggressive (but preferable) "If you . . , if you . . , if you . . " will be welcome everywhere in church worship. It was published in this (the bland) form in *Psalms for Today* and *Songs from the Psalms* (both 1990) to tunes by my *Jubilate* musical colleagues David Peacock ('Dartmeet') and Noël Tredinnick ('Fullness').

While the above is the rationale for the text, the inspiration comes, of course, from Rudyard Kipling's famous poem, '*If*'. After a whole list of strictures ('If . . . ') Kipling asserts the reward of following his advice, "You'll be a man, my son." Not very distant, I thought, from "Blessed is the man." Just for interest, Rudyard Kipling lived and wrote near Burwash in East Sussex, only a few miles across hill and valley from Mayfield where I am writing this commentary now.

Bible reference: Psalm 1.

77.
I'll praise you, Lord
Psalm 138 is a wonderful psalm of personal devotion; confidence in God in whatever situation we find ourselves. We praise God for who he is and

241

what he has done; we are affirmed in our stature before him. The text is also available in plural form: *We'll praise you, Lord*

Bible reference: Psalm 138.

78.

In a stable, in a manger

This translates a Spanish carol and is set to the original tune in *Carol Praise* (published 1987). The opening line is too close for comfort to *O my darling Clementine* ("In a cavern, in a canyon"). American editors have frequently improved my texts (c.f. in particular, *In Christ there is no East or West/in Christ no South or North*), and I'm open to suggestions! Even so, it's not that bad—even rising to truly poetic exhortation in stanza 3. Moreover, is good to have available a translation of another of a European carol.

Bible reference: Luke 2.7.

79.

In Christ there is no east or west, in him no pride of birth *(UK)*

(See also: In Christ there is no east or west, in Christ no South or North.)
Written in 1978 at Bitterne when the East/West consciousness was still at its height. This began as a revision of the well-known hymn by W. A. Dunkerley. It was soon realized that so radical must be the revision that an entirely new hymn might be constructed. The spirit of reconciliation was invoked from the Pauline Epistles, and the spirit of fellowship from the Johannine.

Bible references: Matthew 12.46,   Mark 3.31,   Luke 8.19,
2 Corinthians 5.18,   Galatians 3.28,   Ephesians 2.14,   Colossians 1.20,
Colossians 3.11.

80.

In Christ there is no east or west, in Christ no South or North *(USA)*

(See also: In Christ there is no east or west, in him no pride of birth.)
This began as a North American variant of the 1978 original, published first in *The Canadian Catholic Hymnal:*

In Christ there is no East or West,
in Christ no South or North;
but one great family of love
throughout the whole wide earth.

For God in Christ has made us one
from every land and race,
has reconciled us through the Son
and made us whole by grace.

So brothers, sisters, praise his name
who died to set us free
from sin, division, hate and shame,
from spite and enmity!

In Christ now meet both East and West,
in Christ meet South and North—
one joyful human family
throughout the whole wide earth.

My first reaction was that the revision considerably improved upon my original, which made me want to echo the words of John Ellerton, the author of *The day thou gavest, Lord, is ended*:

> "Anyone who presumes to lay his offering of a song of praise upon the altar, not for his own but for God's glory, cannot be too thankful for the devout, thoughtful and scholarly criticism of those whose object it is to make his work less unworthy of it sacred purpose."

I must have had my eyes closed, however, for it was much later when I noticed that the redactor had missed rhymes in lines 3 of stanzas 1 and 4. 'Love' and 'family' do not rhyme with 'West'! The Canadian improvement is now merged with true rhymes to give the 'USA' version in this book.

Bible references: Matthew 12.46,   Mark 3.31,   Luke 8.19, 2 Corinthians 5.18,   Galatians 3.28,   Ephesians 2.14,   Colossians 1.20, Colossians 3.11.

81.

In majesty and splendor
Psalm 104 is a wonderfully descriptive nature psalm; I mean to do a version for children some time, for whom its pictures would be enthralling. *In majesty and splendor* attempts to cover much of the story and, though I would not write like this now, the existence of the text underlines for me two discoveries. One was theological, and represented by the lines—

> "Yet what are we without you?
> you hide your face, we die:
> so while life lasts, we worship
> and praise you, God most high!"

How much our *every breath* depends on God! Yet there is nothing we can do to stave off our eventual demise; nor the surprise of an early death. So it is right that we should give to God in worship every moment during which he sustains us in life.

The second discovery was how excellent a composer was my colleague Norman Warren who set this text to the exciting performance melody he now calls *Majesty and Splendor*. Norman has subsequently worked with me on the production of several books and more than one operetta.

Bible reference: Psalm 104.

82.

In the darkness of the night
Attempted here is an English counterpart of the Welsh carol; "Yr hen gelynnen". It was prepared for *Carol Praise* (published 1987) and is directed by the sentiments of *Isaiah* 9.

Bible reference: Isaiah 9.2.

83.

In the streets of every city

One of the alarming things about being a member of the *Jubilate* group of writers and composers is that you are liable to be called at any moment with the request to write a text, or compose a tune (unless you are me—no self-respecting *Jubilate* editor *ever* asks me for a tune) for a close deadline. So it was with *In the streets of every city*. David Peacock called me at Mayfield on my day off and asked for this text "by tomorrow". It was for the 1993 UK Baptist Conference, of which he was music director, and it had to include the line "where it matters there you'll find us"—the theme of the conference. Chris Rolinson, another *Jubilate* member was to write the tune. Hence three Anglicans—David, Chris and I—were involved in preparing the theme hymn for a Baptist event—at which the guest speaker was to be the Anglican George Carey, Archbishop of Canterbury. There's ecumenism!

I here and now confess that it was two years later when I noticed that I had lifted a line ('In the streets of every city') and a rhyme (city/pity) from Hugh Sherlock's *Lord thy/your church on earth is seeking*—at least they were from the last verse! Since Hugh Sherlock was good enough to let Michael Saward recast his own original hymn and publish, I trust no-one will resent the loan of a line to me!

The theme of the hymn signals places where the Christian must be found—in the community (witnessing, healing, peace-making), throughout the world (sharing the work of evangelism), at prayer, at communion, at worship.

Chris Rolinson's tune was 'song-style' and adjusted the wording to fit. The text as printed here has yet to find a hymn setting.

Bible references: Genesis 14.8, Isaiah 53.5, Matthew 15.31, Romans 8.23.

84.

Jesus, child of Mary

I was quite pleased with this simple carol when it was completed at the end of a wet and difficult family vacation in Cornwall in 1980 (See: *The brightness of God's glory*). More satisfying was the fact that I had also written a tune rather better than most of my other attempts at composing. I was just in time to submit the text for *Hymns for Today's Church*, only to run into trouble. Michael Baughen was the chairman of our group, and the first line of my carol rang the wrong bells: " . . child of Mary *Baughen*"? The team 'fell about laughing', and in my shyness I quickly withdrew the contribution. Ten years later, I suggested that David Iliff and David Peacock look at it for *Carols for Today* and *Carol Praise* respectively. Both encouraged me to include the text; Norman Warren produced an arrangement of my melody, which I then called 'Hayle' after the seaside village in Cornwall where the words and music had begun to flow.

This carol celebrates the paradox of the 'Lord most high' descending to earth. I remember some theological debate over the second stanza: was it Docetist?

> To this place of pain and fear
> love descends in human guise;
> God in Christ self-emptied here,
>   foolishness most wise.

In the end it was agreed that I had avoided heresy and need not change the text. I had not exactly said *God* was 'in human guise', and I *had* allied myself to the now more acceptable 'kenotic' model, "God in Christ self-emptied". Glad to be acquitted, I was also relieved not to have to alter one of my best ever stanzas!

Bible references: Matthew 27.29,   Mark 15.17,   John 19.2, 1 Corinthians 1.27, Philippians 2.7.

85.
Jesus Christ the Lord is born
An essential part of *Hymns for Today's Church* (published 1980) was to be its careful updating of texts; the words team spent many hours over seven years meeting this challenge. Even then we didn't get it right; another seven years on we produced a radical revision (the second edition, published 1987/8). Very many writers and publisher copyright-holders could see the point of what we were doing and entered into conversation with us about acceptable revision of texts they owned. Only a few were obdurate; among these were the owners of *Unto us a boy is born* in respect of the frequent archaisms in that text. The tune *Puer Nobis* from *Piae Cantiones* (1582) and the Latin and German source texts are, or course non-copyright, so in the end the *Hymns for Today's Church* editorial group opted for a new translation/paraphrase. I agreed to attempt this and the text *Jesus Christ the Lord is born* was the result. I cannot remember if my text emerged from a paraphrase of the German 'Uns ist geborn ein Kindelein', or as a translation of the Latin. In any case it is obviously free representation—picking up suggestions from the Latin text—rather than in strict conformity.

Puer nobis nascitur,
rector angelorum:
in hoc mundo pascitur
Dominus Dominorum.

In prasepe positum
sub foeno asinorum
cognoverunt Dominum
Christum, Regem Coelorum.

Hunc Herodes timuit
magno cum tremore;
in infantes irruit
hos caedens in furore.

Qui natus ex Maria
die hodierna:
duc nos, tua gratia,
ad gaudia superna.

'Te salvator A et O,'
cantemus in choro;
cantemus in organo:
'Benedicamus Domino.'

In the course of writing, one or two less likely rhymes emerged: maternal/eternal, anger/danger. These were indeed creative days! I do also remember being challenged about the presumption that there were *three* wise men; was this not the evidence of Christmas cards rather than Scripture? Eventually, fundamentalism won the day, and I was allowed my line: "Soon shall come the wise men three". At least, by assigning this event to the future I was not compounding the crib error—with the magi in the stable, along with Mary, Joseph, two donkeys, three sheep, a cow, six angels and a Sunday School teacher.

Bible references: Psalm 150.6, Micah 5.2, Matthew 2.1, Matthew 2.1, Matthew 2.2, Matthew 2.13, Matthew 2.18, Luke 2, Luke 2.1, Luke 2.12, Luke 2.13, John 11, Romans 5.17, Romans 6.4, 2 Timothy 1.10, Hebrews 9.14, 1 John 3.14.

86.
Jesus, hope of every nation
This began life as one of my early attempts to 'lighten' the Anglican canticles. I rendered *Nunc Dimittis* somewhat artlessly as:

'Let me now depart in peace
to my passing reconciled;
thankful, e'er my life should cease,
to have seen the holy Child.

'Jesus, hope of every nation
dawn of God's eternal day;
sent to offer full* salvation—
he himself shall light the way.

'Lord, your servants long have waited
trusting you to keep your word;
now our faith is vindicated

for these eyes have seen the Lord'

Glory be to God the Father,
glory be to God the Son,
with the everlasting Spirit:
praise for ever God as One!

*Originally 'men'.

. . and it was published in *Psalm Praise* (1973) to a Perry tune which had a 'plainsong' feel, arranged by Christian Strover. *Let me now depart in peace* was not felt to be adequate by other editors. The opening line, which severely linked it to the traditional canticle, and the first person singular idiom, made certain that it would never be sung in any other context. Keen to preserve one of my few tunes, I set to work on the text, turning it into a more general advent hymn by the time of publication of *Hymns for Today's Church* (1981). The doxology derives from the canticle version, but serves here as the greeting announced in stanza 3; seasonally appropriate since it begins with the angels' hymn, "Glory in the highest heaven . ."

Bible references: Isaiah 11.10, Isaiah 41.14, Isaiah 42.6, Isaiah 49.6, Jeremiah 14.8, Jeremiah 17.13, Matthew 4.15, Luke 2.29, Luke 2.29, Acts 13.47, Acts 26.23, Romans 15.12, Revelation 19.13.

87.
Jesus is our refuge

Jesus is our refuge is based on *Dies es nuestro,* a Chilean melody—hence the irregular meter—and was prepared at the request of David Peacock as music director of the 1995 World Baptist Congress in Argentina. It is not in fact a translation or paraphrase, but the reliance on *Psalm 46* and *Revelation* 1 was inspired by the original Spanish.

Bible references: Psalm 46, Matthew 24.30, Matthew 26.64, Mark 13.26, Mark 14.62, Luke 21.26, Revelation 1.7.

88.
Jesus, Redeemer, come
As the 'established' church in the UK, the Church of England conducts many more marriage ceremonies than might be suggested by its regular membership. Additionally, since the Church was in this industry long before the state legislated for secular weddings, the Church of England clergy are legal officers in regard to marriages, and act entirely independently of the secular state 'registrars' of marriage. In 1980, the *Alternative Service Book* gave the Church of England an authorized contemporary language marriage service. Norman Warren and I responded with *The Wedding Book* (published 1989). In this we drew together the *ASB 1980* marriage service, suitable hymns in revised format, incidental music for organ etc in simple format, and one or two popular solo pieces.

For many years *Ave Maria,* in either Bach/Gounod or Schubert version, had been popular at weddings as a recital piece. Non-catholic ministers were none too happy at this but, provided it was sung in Latin (which meant few could understand it) and provided it was done when they were in the vestry with the couple and their immediate family signing the registers, they tended to wince and bear it. It was agreed that I should write an English (and protestant!) version, so that there might be some comprehensible verbal content by which the congregation might be blessed. Hence this text.

The book was launched in Westminster Abbey, and I well remember Norman and Yvonne Warren's daughter Ruth, who has a delightful voice, singing this text to the Bach/Gounod melody for the first time in public from the organ loft on the great screen across the Abbey.

Bible references: Proverbs 18.24,   Isaiah 6.7,   Romans 5.10, 2 Corinthians 5.15, Ephesians 2.8, Ephesians 3.17, 1 Thessalonians 5.10, 1 Peter 3.15, 2 Peter 1.19, Revelation 1.5.

89.
Jesus, Redeemer, Mary's Child
See *Jesus, Redeemer, come* for the explanation and origins of this text written to the music of Franz Schubert, *Ave Maria.*

Bible references: Isaiah 53.7,   Isaiah 66.2,   2 Corinthians 5.20, Philippians 2.8, Colossians 1.22, James 4.10, 1 Peter 3.15.

90.
Jesus, Savior, holy Child
Aware of the popularity of the *Rocking Carol,* we wanted it for our carol
books, yet we felt that the prevailing English text was far too sentimental
for adult worship and patronizing to children.
"Little Jesus, sweetly sleep . .
we will rock you . .
we will bring you a coat of fur . . etc."

So we examined the original in translation—only to find that this was even
more sentimental; a subjective judgment, of course but, I think, one from
which few worship leaders/planners would dissent!

My hope is that *Jesus, Savior, holy Child* will make the *Rocking Carol*
melody usable in the context of adult Christmas worship, either as a choir
piece, or as a congregational carol.

Bible references: Luke 2.7,   Luke 2.14,   2 Corinthians 8.9,
2 Corinthians 8.9, Philippians 2.7.

91.
Journey to Bethlehem
In 1987 Norman Warren and I published a little dance operetta for
Christmas. It was called *Welcome your King* and this was one of the songs.
The carol was subsequently published in *Carol Praise.*

Bible reference: Matthew 2.9.

92.
Let the desert sing
Written when I was ill in bed during time of the evening service at Bitterne
in 1979. There's nothing very profound about it, but the stanzas are really
three lines long (not six) with the meter as 10.11.11 (approximately!)
which is asking a lot of composers. The various published attempts at a
tune have been unexciting! Between first draft and publication there was
no change at all—which is unique among my hymns. Later, however, the
original stanza three, line three, 'and the voice of the dumb shall shout
aloud' was changed to 'and the voice of the silent shout aloud' because of
the American colloquial use of 'dumb' to mean stupid.

Bible references: Isaiah 35,   Isaiah 35.1,   Isaiah 41.18,   Isaiah 51.11,
Matthew 11.5, Matthew 15.30, Mark 7.37, Luke 7.21, John 9.1, Acts 3.1.

93.
Lift up your hearts to the Lord
Psalm Praise (1973) contains the original for this hymn version of *Psalm
98.* The first line then read *'Sound loud the trumpet and strings'. Psalm 98*
was also deployed as a regular Canticle in the *Book of Common Prayer
(1662)* service of 'Evening Prayer', and hence the hymn's appearance in

the canticle section of *Psalm Praise*. When the *Jubilate* team were working on *Psalm Praise* (published 1983) we at first concluded that rhyme didn't matter. Poets in our age are less insistent upon rhyme and; after years of 'stuffing' words into cathedral chant, who among our intended users was going to care about the lack of rhyme in metrical versions? For the impatient majority of young people, at least, anything was going to be better than the obscurities and apparent idiosyncrasies of pointed Coverdale psalms. However, as time went by and the most fluent of us, Timothy Dudley-Smith, went on rhyming, we reverted to standard rhyme schemes. This text dates from the earlier period.

Bible references: Psalm 98.1, Lamentations 3.41, Matthew 24.31, 1 Corinthians 15.52, Ephesians 5.12, 1 Thessalonians 4.16.

94.
Lift your heart and raise your voice
I used to remark that any writer who ended a Christmas carol with 'Gloria' was nigh-on sure of finding a competent arranger to provide a musical setting. These words, written for *Carols for Today* (1990), evoked the marvelous tune *Marston St. Lawrence* from Paul Edwards, formerly a chorister at St. Paul's Cathedral in London.

It is a carol of contrasts between heaven and earth, riches and poverty, wisdom and foolishness, power and pain, kingship and sacrifice, pomp and humility, humanity and angels.

Bible references: Luke 2.16, 1 Corinthians 1.30.

95.
Like a mighty river flowing
When in 1981 I moved from the bustle of Southampton to the serenity of Eversley in the countryside of north Hampshire, I wrote this hymn as an act of thanksgiving. Most of it was completed in the garden of Eversley Rectory on a wonderful day in late spring. Each stanza moves from the visual to the abstract, the beauty of the natural creation to the inner world of prayer. Each stanza resolves into the conclusion of the *Philippians* 4 exhortation: "By prayer and petition . . present your requests to God . . and the peace of God, which transcends all understanding, will guard your heart and your mind in Christ Jesus."

In each stanza a specific experience and location is remembered:
'a mighty river' recalls my first ever flight which took me over a south Devon estuary—a wonderful expanse of water for a young boy.

'a flower in beauty growing' was a special rose given to us by a caring and prayerful family when we left our first post—it was planted in our second garden and gave us great joy.

'*the hills serene and even*' were the sweeping hills of southern England; most especially the South Downs and the Berkshire Ridgeway.

'*the tall trees softly swaying*' were the trees behind Eversley Rectory as I wrote the hymn.

'*the lips of silent praying*' were those of a young woman in church one afternoon—making her peace with God; so reminiscent of the *1 Samuel* 1.13 description of Hannah in the temple at Shiloh:
"Hannah was praying in her heart, and her lips were moving but her voice was not heard."

'*the morning sun ascended*' was the experience of standing on Butser Hill and watching the sun mysteriously emerge from the mist. Butser is a famous beacon hill and site of iron age settlement—now part of the Queen Elizabeth Park in Hampshire.

'*the scents of evening blended*'—I recalled the sensation as a child of leaning out of an upstairs window and being fascinated by the mix of scents on an early summer evening.

'*the azure ocean swelling*'—I was always fascinated by the sea—to go to sea I am sure would have been my alternative vocation. This recollection was probably of an early 'voyage' from Esbjerg in Denmark to Whitstable in Kent on a small freighter.

This hymn has been popularly used on television in the United Kingdom, often chosen where the town or city from which the service comes is situated on a river. Sometimes it is sung to *Quem pastores*, but more often to Noël Tredinnick's evocative *Old Yeavering*.

Bible references: Genesis 5.22,   Genesis 24.45,   1   Samuel 1.13,   1 Samuel 20.42,   1   Samuel 23.18,   Job 29.4,   Job 35.5,   Psalm 119.165, Psalm 121.1,   Psalm 147.8,   Isaiah 26.3,   Isaiah 48.18,   Isaiah 66.12, Luke 7.47, Philippians 4.7, Hebrews 11.5.

96.
Lord Jesus Christ, invited guest
Lord Jesus Christ was written in 1981 at the suggestion of the *Jubilate* team when permission to update the wedding hymn *O perfect Love*, then popular in the UK, was refused. *Lord Jesus Christ*, being in the same meter, could then be sung to the tune of the original. Apart from that, there is no connection between the two hymns—except, of course, their wedding context. The first and last lines allude to the *John* 2 wedding in Cana of Galilee; in stanza 3, the words 'in joy', 'in sorrow', 'in pleasure', in 'pain' echo traditional wedding vows:

I, N, take you, *N*,
to be my wife/husband,
to have and to hold

from this day forward;
for better, for worse,
for richer, for poorer,
in sickness and in health
to love and to cherish,
till death us do part,
according to God's holy law;
and this is my solemn vow.

Bible references: John 2.1, John 4.46.

97.
Lord Jesus, for my sake you come
As with *The hands of Christ,* this hymn is anatomical in so far as eyes, tears, face, head and hands are mentioned. It was an early text in the first writing period for *Hymns for Today's Church.* It was also a period when evangelical Christians in England were becoming once again socially aware; hence stanza 2.

As to Bible allusions, the following may elude the casual reader: stanza 2, 'Your eyes seek out' alludes to *Luke* 19.10 ('The Son of Man came to seek and to save what was lost') etc.; stanza 3, 'Your face is set' to *Luke* 9.51 ('Jesus . . set his face to go to Jerusalem). Stanza 4 'You never grasped at selfish gain' alludes to *Philippians* 2.6.

Bible references: Matthew 27.29, Mark 15.17, Luke 9.51, Luke 19.10, John 19.2, John 19.30, Philippians 2.6.

98.
Lord Jesus, let these eyes of mine
Written in 1978 at Bitterne, this hymn was subject to much early criticism and, I hope, improvement. The 'whispering voice' allusion in stanza 2 is to Elijah in *1 Kings 19.11ff* ('The Lord was not in the fire. But after the fire came a gentle whisper'). 'To think upon the good I find' in stanza 3 connects with *Philippians* 4.8 ('think about these things'). *Lord Jesus, let these eyes of mine* is about the dedication of all our powers in the service of God. I asked for it to be used at my service of induction as Vicar of Tonbridge.

Bible references: 1 Kings 19.11, Jeremiah 1.9.

99.
Lord of love, you come to bless
David Peacock, in the process of editing *World Praise (2)* for the 1995 World Baptist Congress in Argentina, asked me to provide English words to this New Zealand Maori tune. Although this is not in any way a translation or paraphrase, as far as can I remember I drew my theme from the subject addressed in the original text. *Romans 3.21-26* was the

251

Scripture inspiration, but there are obvious references to the gospel stories of the passion of Jesus.

The third stanza begins with an illusion to a sentence in the *Third Eucharistic Prayer* of the Church of England's *Alternative Service Book 1980* concerning Jesus' sacrifice on Calvary: "He opened wide his arms for us on the cross". That phrasing may well have originated with a famous hymn-writer, Charles Coffin (1676-1749), Rector of the University of Paris. He published in 1736 his *Hymni Sacri*, a collection of one hundred Latin hymns, many of which were incorporated into the *Paris Breviary* for that year. The second stanza of Charles Coffin's hymn *Labente jam solis rota* reads:

O Christe, dum fixus cruci
expandis orbi bracchia
amare da crucem; tuo
da nos in amplexu mori.

Bible references: Mark 15, Luke 23, Romans 3.

100.
Lord, you are love
Although some members of the *Jubilate* group were pioneers of the contemporary Christian song idiom in the UK—hence the ultimately influential and formative *Youth Praise* and *Jesus Praise*—not all of them saw things that way. Indeed, Michael Baughen, who was primarily responsible for *Youth Praise,* and for a long while led *Jubilate,* was none too happy when Norman Warren and David Peacock proposed and published *Jesus Praise.* Other *Jubilate* writers—notably Paul Wigmore—pleaded for us to write songs "with content" to balance out what they saw as the banal influence of many of the worship songs. *Lord, you are love* was one of my own few attempts to write something in the worship song idiom. Of course, most worship song lyrics are written by the composer of the melody. This in itself may be a great loss, since few originators of songs combine words- and music-writing skills.

Bible reference: 1 John 4.16.

101.
Lullaby, little Jesus
Written for *Carols for Today* to the Polish carol tune *Jezus malusienki*. It was eventually displaced in that volume by Paul Wigmore's text *Such a night in Bethlehem*, to the same tune, only to reappear in *Carol Praise*.

Bible references: Luke 2.7.

102.
Mary and Joseph, praise with them

In 1987 Norman Warren and I published a little dance operetta for Christmas. It was called *Welcome your King* and this was one of the songs. The carol subsequently appeared in *Carol Praise*.

Bible reference: Luke 2.20.

103.

Mary sang a song

Mary sang a song was part of my early attempt to simplify the Anglican *Book of Common Prayer* canticles—here the *Magnificat*. I retained the word 'magnify' in the first line to identify the song, whereas I would normally now shun such an archaism. 'Magnify' in secular English now commonly describes the operation of a converging lens or, in the abstract, to 'magnify' someone's faults—a negative connotation. It never stands in for the word 'praise', except in religious circles; it has therefore become exclusive.

There is a 'fun' musical setting of *Mary sang a song*—an arrangement for vocal soloist, supporting choir, piano and saxophone. Smiles and applause greeted this setting as we used it for a nationwide live television broadcast on the Sunday before Christmas, 1994. The arrangement by Richard Walshaw is of a considerably adapted version of Peter Brown's published tune.

Bible references: Luke 1.46, Luke 1.46, Luke 1.46.

104.

May the Lord God hear you pray

This psalm is a comprehensive benediction, and the hymn version attempts to reflect this type of prayer. It was devised for *Psalms for Today*.

There is also a song variant of this text, which appears in *Songs from the Psalms*:

> May the Lord God hear your prayer,
> may his name protect you always;
> may he meet you in his house,
> lifting up your heart in worship.
>
> May he grant your true desire,
> may he make your plans successful
> may he give you all you need,
> causing everyone to thank him.
>
> Now we know the Lord can save,
> now we trust this world no longer,
> now we see God answers prayer—
> praise him now for all his mercy!

Bible reference: Psalm 20.

105.
My faithful shepherd is the Lord
The Scottish metrical psalm *The Lord's my shepherd* became immensely popular in the United Kingdom after being sung to the tune *Crimond* at the wedding of the Duke of York and Lady Elizabeth Bowes-Lyon. They were eventually to become King George VI and his Queen Elizabeth. In the process of revising hymns for *Hymns for Today's Church,* the *Jubilate* team realized that no modern language version of this hymn was going to satisfy the Christian public; any change would have to be too radical.

The chosen alternative was to create an original parallel modern language version. Chris Idle took one route and wrote *The Lord my shepherd knows my name* to the same meter. It was published first in Scripture Union's *Songs of Worship).* I took the other route, and wrote this hymn to Long Meter. Mine did not appear until *Church Family Worship* (1986)—alongside Chris' version.

Bible reference: Psalm 23.

106.
No sorrow, no mourning, no crying *(Raise up your kingdom)*
Created for *World Praise 2 (*1995) to be set to the tune *Um pouco alem de presente;* this is not a translation, but a song representation of the themes of *Revelation* chapters 21—23.

Bible references: Revelation 21, Revelation 22, Revelation 23

107.
Not the grandeur of the mountains
One summer in the 1980's, Beatrice and I took our two children, Helen and Simon, to Scotland. For two weeks we lived among the mountains in and around Skye. We observed, and I photographed, mountains and clouds, lochs and mists—and especially the unforgettable sight of the clouds flowing over the straight of sea between Skye and the mainland. Hence this hymn, written in two styles—one echoing the worship of the great Keswick Convention of years gone by; a similar experience of hills and natural beauty. Another, self-consciously a tribute to Timothy Dudley-Smith who taught me so much in the early days of working together for *Psalm Praise.* Timothy groups negatives—resolving them into a positive conclusion with satisfying effect.

Bible references: Psalm 8.4, Psalm 36.7, Psalm 86.15, Psalm 111.8, Psalm 118.3, Psalm 119.165, Psalm 136.26, Isaiah 26.3, Ephesians 3.19, 2 John 1.2.

108.
Now evening comes to close the day

This was conceived as an evening hymn without attachment to any particular original text. It's similarity to sentiments expressed in *Te lucis ante terminum* (the canticle *Before the ending of the day*) nevertheless impressed me sufficiently to include it in the canticle section of *Psalms for Today*. My colleagues accepted it probably because of the interesting tune from Peter White! The text of *Te lucis* below will probably serve to show readers with Latin how far from the original is *Now evening comes to close the day*. Nevertheless, I think all would agree there are resonances. *Te lucis* is a hymn of great antiquity, found in the earliest Ambrosian manuscripts—though this is not to say it was by St. Ambrose himself. Liturgically, it comes down to us through the service of *Compline* in the western church.

Te lucis ante terminum,
rerum creator, poscimus
ut solita clementia
sis praesul ad custodiam.

procul recedant somnia
et noctium phantasmata,

hostemque nostrum comprime,
ne polluantur corpora.

praesta, Pater omnipotens,
per Jesum Christum Dominum,
qui tecum in perpetuum
regnat cum sancto Spiritu.

Bible references: Psalm 141.2, Philippians 4.8, Colossians 3.1.

109.
Now through the grace of God
The words editors of *Hymns for Today's Church*, noticed a lack of contemporary hymns on baptism. This was one my attempts to meet that need—in parallel with other contributions by Timothy Dudley-Smith, Chris Idle and Michael Saward—eventually all were printed. *Now through the grace of God* is in Common Meter and therefore readily accessible. The textual base is a mixture of *Romans* and *Hebrews* (see below).

Bible references: Matthew 28.19, Romans 6.4-5, Hebrews 7.25.

110.
O bless the God of Israel
(See: *Blest be the God of Israel*)
This was written as *O bless the God of Israel* for *Psalm Praise* and published in that form in 1973. Subsequently it was revised and improved in versions with both first lines. In the United States, Hal H Hopson wrote *Merle's Tune* for this text, and the combination appears in various hymnals.

Bible references: Judges 5.3, 1 Samuel 25.32, 2 Samuel 22.29, 1 Kings 8.15, 2 Chronicles 6.4, Psalm 18.28, Psalm 72.18, Psalm 106.48, Isaiah 61.1, Matthew 1.1, Matthew 4.16, Luke 1.61, Luke 1.68, Luke 7.16, Luke 24.21.

111.
O bless the Lord, my soul

This was one of two texts I wrote for *Psalm Praise*—the other one was published. *O bless the Lord etc.* appeared, rescued by a John Barnard tune, in *Psalms for Today*. If there's any virtue here, it's in simplicity, in the matching of the first and the last lines of the hymn, and in the turning point at stanza 6: 'Yet what you give, O sovereign Lord, your power can take away'. I remember being struck as I wrote this hymn by the psalmist's expression of the impermanence of life, and that truth is never very far from my consciousness. In the presence of a sovereign God, the ultimate consequence of being aware of our mortality must be humility and awe.

Bible reference: Psalm 104.

112.
O Christ of all the ages, come
Every so often in my writing, I would lapse into a mystical mood and have to be hauled out by my *Jubilate* friends! This was usually when I was pursuing internal rhymes, as here: 'fear' 'near', 'match' 'watch', 'tearing' 'caring', 'morning' 'dawning', 'days' 'praise'. Written in 1978 to the tune 'Gonfalon Royal' (a gonfalon is a banner, often with streamers, hung from a crossbar) for the opening of a new year. It anticipates Lent, Passiontide and Easter. Typical periods of time are placed strategically throughout the stanzas: ages, months, years, moments, hours, days, morning, years, ages; days, months, years, eternity.

Bible references: Genesis 1.14, Isaiah 53.12, 1 Peter 2.24.

113.
O come, Christians, wonder
Here is a carol based on a Welsh original. I do believe this is a reasonable versification of the English prose translation made by a Welsh friend. I confess that I have now lost the paraphrase—and the friend. Since the Welsh tune was not used in the first publication in *Carol Praise*, I have not been able to trace the text by association, either. Any help from a reader would be gratefully received!

Bible references: Psalm 34.14, Ephesians 2.5, 1 Peter 3.11.

114.
O come, our world's Redeemer, come
From the Latin text of St. Ambrose: *Veni Redemptor gentium*

Veni, Redemptor gentium,
ostende partum Virginis:
miretur omne sacculum:
talis decet partus Deum.

Non ex virili semine
sed mystico spiramine
verbum Dei factust caro
fructusque ventris floruit.

Alvus tumescit Virginis,
claustrum pudoris permanet;
vexilla virtutum micant:
versatur in templo Deus.

Procedat e thalamo suo,
pudoris aula regiâ,
geminae gigas substantiae,

alacris ut currat viam!

virtute firmans perpeti.

Egressus ejus a Patre,
regressus ejus ad Patrem;
excursus usque ad inferos,
recursus ad sedem Dei.

Praesaepe jam fulget tuum,
lumenque nox spirat suum;
quod nulla vox interpolet
fideque jugi luceat.

Aequalis aeterno Patri
carnis trophaeo cingere,
infirma nostri corporis

Bible references: Luke 1.31, Luke 1.42, Luke 2.7, John 1.14, Philippians 2.7, Revelation 22.20.

115.

O God beyond all praising

Written for the Gustav Holst's melody 'Thaxted' (normally associated in the UK with the ode 'I vow to thee my country') in response to a call for alternative words that would be more appropriate for Christian worship. It is a carefully constructed hymn of contrasts—even paradox—throughout. Allusions to the Anglican liturgy, both in its spirit ('We do not presume to come to this your table...'), and in word ('We lift our hearts before you', 'joyful duty', 'sacrifice of praise') are intended to make the hymn useful at Holy Communion. Stanza 1, line 4 stands as an acknowledgment of Timothy Dudley Smith's help and encouragement to me ('...without number' is a device beloved of 'TDS'); Stanza 3, lines 3 and 4 reflect my remembered determination of youthful days to overcome acute disappointment and personal loss ('we'll triumph through our sorrows and rise to bless you still').

Stanza 2 was a later addition by request of Richard Proulx, and *G.I.A. Publications* in Chicago, who wanted to produce a special anthem setting. It was to be set liturgically for Sunday with a denominationally prescribed reading (*1 Corinthians* 15). In the eventual Concertato, published by *G.I.A* in 1988 ad the choir sining the optional verse.

On the whole, the tune is fairly 'heavy' and my own preference would be for the hymn normally to be sung without this middle stanza—certainly in the communion context.

Bible references: Job 13.15, Job 13.15, Psalm 8.4, Psalm 27.4, Psalm 50.2, Psalm 116.17, Psalm 130.5, Psalm 130.5, Ecclesiastes 12.13, Lamentations 3.41, Lamentations 3.41, Hebrews 13.15, James 1.17, James 1.17.

116.

O God, we thank you that your name

This is another of those psalms that nobody else wanted to versify. Its imagery is obscure and, in places, vengeful. My intention was to distill the truths from it for worship; hence, *O God, we thank you that your name*

Bible reference: Psalm 75.

117.

O gracious Lord, be near me

Written for *Psalm Praise,* and revised for *Psalms for Today.* The *Psalm Praise* version read:

O Lord, be gracious to me,
my soul cries out, 'How long?'
When will you turn in mercy
and save your child from wrong?

'Shall lips that you have given
sing praises from the dead?
Return, O Lord, enliven—
in love lift up my head.'

Despair my mind was keeping
and sorrows filled my eyes:
but God has heard my weeping,
and now he will arise!

My original tune suffered a radical adjustment such as I have been wont to give to other people's words. It came back from Norman Warren as *Psalm Praise 65. Psalms for Today* set the revised text to *Gauntlet,* though the original text had considerable use to *Kocher*—a mournful tune, if ever there was one. *Kocher* is traditionally used in the U.K. to 'O happy band of pilgrims'. But the plaintive aspect of *Kocher* is eminently suited to *Psalm 6.*

Bible reference: Psalm 6.

118.

O Jesus, my Lord, how sweetly you lie

This version follows *O Jesulein süss, O Jesulein mild,* notably set to music by S. Scheidt (c. 1650).

O Jesulein süss! o Jesulein mild!
Deines Vaters Willen hast du erfüllt;
bist kommen aus dem Himmelreich,
uns armen Menschen worden gleich
o Jesulein süss! o Jesulein mild!

O Jesulein süss, o Jesulein mild!
Deins du zahlst für uns all unser Schuld,
und bringst uns hin deins Vaters Huld,
o Jesulein süss! o Jesulein mild!

O Jesulein süss! o Jesulein mild!
Mit Freuden hast du die Welt erfüllt,
du kommst herab vom Himmelssaal,
und trostst uns in dem Jammerthal,
o Jesulein süss! o Jesulein mild!

O Jesulein süss! o Jesulein mild!
Sei unser Schirm und unser Schild,

wir bitten durch dein Geburt im Stall,
beschütz uns all vor Sündenfall,
o Jesulein süss! o Jesulein mild!

O Jesulein süss! o Jesulein mild!
Du bist der Lieb ein Ebenbild,
zünd an in uns der Liebe Flamm,
dass wir dich lieben allzusamm,
o Jesulein süss! o Jesulein mild!

O Jesulein süss, o Jesulein mild!
Hilf, dass wir thun alls, was du willt,
was unser ist, ist Alles dein,
ach lass uns dir befohlen seyn,
o Jesulein süss! o Jesulein mild!

Schemelli, 1736

Bible references: Psalm 23.4,   Song   of   Songs 8.6,   Luke 2.7,
2 Corinthians 8.9.

119.
O Lord, come quickly when I call
This version of *Psalm 141* was written directly for *Psalms for Today*. I like
to think that *Psalm* 141.8, 'My eyes are fixed on you, Sovereign Lord,'
might have inspired *Hebrews* 12.2, 'Let us fix our eyes on Jesus, the author
and perfecter of our faith.' And *Psalm 141*.3, 'Set a guard upon my mouth,
keep watch over the door of my lips,' is surely not unconnected with *James
1.26,* ' . . a tight rein upon the tongue'.

Bible reference: Psalm 141, James 1.21, Hebrews 12.2

120.
O Lord, my rock, to you I cry
Psalm 28 has as its central theme 'God as the Rock and defence of his
people'. But it is also a psalm about prayer. The psalmist's prayer for
mercy, which begins in verse 1, is answered in verse 6. God has heard his
cry and his heart leaps for joy. This is the hymn text as originally written,
but see the next . . .

Bible reference: Psalm 28.

121.
O Lord, my rock, to you I cry (Variant)
In *Hymns for Today's Church* and in *Psalms for Today* we frequently chose
to write to suitable 'folk' tunes, contending that their ubiquity proved their
value. Obviously, we tried to match the atmosphere of words and music.
David Iliff, as music editor of *Psalms for Today,* suggested I look at the
English traditional tune *The Turtle Dove* as a vehicle for my draft text for
Psalm 28; accordingly I adjusted the text very slightly. Subsequently, we
discovered that *The Turtle Dove* had a 'collection copyright' and that the
agents of the collector's estate were unwilling to let us pay royalties for the
melody 'pro rata' in the book. In other words, they wanted more than the
proportion of the income from sales than equal division would allow. After
some research, David Iliff discovered a compromise, a Somerset folk song
in the public domain, very similar to the desired 'Turtle Dove'. We had to
content ourselves with this in *Psalms for Today*, since when the proprietors
have become more amenable, and it may well be that we can at last use *The
Turtle Dove* to set this text.

Bible reference: Psalm 28.

122.

O Lord, our Lord, how wonderful
Written by request of staff at the Church Pastoral Aid Society for the
official opening by Arcbishop George Carey of their new premises at Royal
Leamington Spa. *(See notes to* 'One thing I know', *and* 'See him lying on a
bed of straw'). This was a further attempt at a song-style presentation of
the psalm.

Bible reference: Psalm 8.

123.

O Lord, our Lord, your beauty fills
Such a beautiful and evocative psalm simply invites versification. Many
have done it successfully. This was one of my later attempts, never
published so far as I am aware.

Bible reference: Psalm 8.

124.

O Lord, the God who saves me
Originally written for, and published in *Psalm Praise,* this psalm text re-
emerged in *Psalms for Today.* 'Do those who are dead rise up and praise
you?' is the plaintive cry on the lips of the psalmist—a question which
needs answering. Wouldn't God prefer us alive? Hence the Christian
response which comes in the last stanza.

Bible reference: Psalm 88.

125.

O people, listen—hear God's wisdom
I find these long-lined stanzas most enjoyable to write; and they are good to
sing. Norman Warren provided a delightful melody (*Wharfdale*), with a
'plainsong' feel. I hope this will make an arrangement and be suitable for a
choir one day. 'Man, despite his riches, does not endure'—this psalm
precisely summarizes the human predicament, but also has hope: 'God will
redeem my life from the grave; he will surely take me to himself'. Such a
foretaste of resurrection theology is rare in the Psalter. I try, in the text, to
contrast these two truths, about mortality and resurrection.

Bible reference: Psalm 49.

126.

O praise the Lord, the mighty God
I am not sure which came first—this text, or *O people, listen.* I suspect, the
latter. Fortunately, Norman Warren's haunting melody, *Wharfdale,* also fits
this one like a glove. It is sufficiently evocative of Hebrew ballad to carry
this version of the song of Zechariah, which became the *Book of Common
Prayer* canticle *Benedictus.* Of the two texts I far prefer *O people, listen;*
and it is unlikely that I could replace my other Benedictus, *Blest be the God
of Israel* in the USA.

Bible reference: Luke 1.61.

127.
On a night when all the world
Written for the tune of *The twelve days of Christmas,* this carol tells the St. Luke's Gospel Christmas story—as against the fantasic gifts in the traditional song—thus making another folk tune usable in worship. Nearly all of the tune *The twelve days of Christmas* is in the public domain; only the melody to the one phrase 'five gold rings' is copyright (*Stainer & Bell*). In order to publish the text of *On a night* to the carol tune without incurring defeating royalty obligations all we had to do was to remove a slur and change a note!

All who know *The twelve days of Christmas* will remember how the story builds up; so, to relate the nativity everything has to be in sequence and there is very little room for maneuver, with short phrases too. There is one desperately unsatisfactory line, 'Sheep were reclining' which never fails to bring mirth to my friends and critics alike. Fortunately, the item is light-hearted, and I always reply that I follow the wisdom of the Amish people. When creating their quilts and other works of art, they have traditionally included a pattern mistake—because 'only God is perfect'!

Bible references: Luke 2.7, Ephesians 2.4.

128.
One thing I know, that Christ has healed
The *Church Pastoral Aid Society* is an Anglican mission agency helping churches to evangelize, teach and pastor. It was founded in 1836, and continues today under the patronage of Her Majesty Queen Elizabeth II, and the presidency of the Archbishops of Canterbury, York, Wales and Ireland. I was asked to write this hymn for the society's third jubilee celebration in 1986. Subsequently (but not as a consequence of writing the hymn!) I have had the honor of being the society's Chairman of Council.

The structure of the hymn is clear; being based on the resolve to unity of purpose: 'One . .' in the Bible texts below.

Stanza 1: The Pharisees ask the man born blind how he received his sight. The question him about Jesus, whom they describe as "a sinner". The man eventually replies, "Whether he is a sinner or not, I don't know. One thing I do know. I was blind and now I see." (*John* 9.25).

Stanza 2: The substance of the stanza is Paul praying about a weakness—anxiety, disability or illness, no-one really knows—he describes as "a thorn in my flesh". "Three times," he says, "I pleaded with the Lord to take it away." The Lord's response to Paul is, "My grace is sufficient for you, for my strength is made perfect in weakness". However, I suspect that the inspiration for the stanza was *Psalm 27.4*:

"One thing I ask of the Lord . . ." Had I remembered where this expression came from I might well have developed the psalm text as the final stanza, since it's prayer continues " . . that I may dwell in the house of the Lord for ever" etc.

Stanza 3: Is Philippians 3. I was especially impressed by an American archaeological discovery made in May 1980. Archaeologists, excavating in Corinth unearthed one of the earliest stadia ever found and discovered fresh evidence on the way races were contested. The starting line was curved, not straight, which suggested that the finish was not a line but a point. This illuminates St. Paul's analogy when he says, literally, "I do not consider myself yet to have taken hold of it . . but I reach out for the marker, to gain the prize" (*Philippians* 3.13, 14) I imagine the winning athlete seizing the wand (rather than breasting the tape) as the token of his victory, and with it claiming the prize—for which he was called up in to the stand where sat the president of the games—"the prize of the upward call" (*Philippians* 3. 14).

Stanza 4: Not having recourse to *Psalm* 27.4 (see above), and recalling the several 'one's' of *Ephesians* 4.5, I settled for that passage as the basis for my finale. I don't think I would now change it, since it seems to work well enough.

Bible references: John 9.25,   2 Corinthians 12.9,   Ephesians 4.5, Philippians 3.13.

129.
Only the fool will say
"The fool has said in his heart" (*Psalm 14*.1 and *Psalm 53*.1*)* is not an opening line to excite hymn writers! Nevertheless, I find such problems a challenge, which is probably why I tend to pick up the 'left-over' jobs! I notice that *Psalm* 14 fell to my lot in preparation for *Psalm Praise* (1973)—a different version, not printed in this collection since it was song-style and not special.

The text is really four lines per stanza, and the meter 10.10.10.10. The words have been set to music in contrasting styles by Paul Edwards in *Psalms for Today* and by Christopher Norton in *Songs from the Psalms*.

Bible references: Psalms 14, Psalm 53.

130.
Praise him, praise him, praise him
Based on Psalm 148 and written in 1970 for *Psalm Praise*, the text was slightly adjusted for use in *Hymns for Today's Church*. It was written to the tune Nicaea, but became better known to the tune *St. Helens* by Kenneth Coates, the vicar of St. Helens, Lancashire, under whom I served as curate 1965-1968. This was a triumph of cooperation, since we

harmonized much better as writer and composer than ever we did as curate and vicar!

Bible references: Psalm 148, Psalm 148, Matthew 24.35, Mark 13.31, Luke 16.17, Luke 21.33.

131.
Praise the Father, God of justice
The hymn was written in response to a request for 'praise' texts with a Trinitarian base early during the preparation of *Hymns for Today's Church*. Accordingly, the stanzas treat God as Father, Son and Holy Spirit, with the fourth stanzas summarizing and unifying the persons of the trinity and our experience of God as Three-in-One. It was, in fact, first published in *Songs of Worship* (1980).

Bible references: Isaiah 48.18, Isaiah 66.2, Isaiah 66.12, Romans 6.4, Ephesians 4.16, Colossians 2.19.

132.
Rejoice with heart and voice
This version of *Gaudete* was prepared for *Carols for Today* and *Carol Praise*. The tune and text are medieval, but popularized (at least in the UK) in the present century by the pop group *Steel Eye Span*. This made it very much a candidate for the carol books which as editors we hoped would meet the churches' need for new but recognizable material for a season when one third of the British public attended some sort of carol celebration. In writing the carol I felt that the use of the Latin '-ation' ending was entirely appropriate, since I was translating Latin. It also met the constraints of rhythm particularly well. As with the French carol *Dans cette étable*, 'beginnings are endings'; to be true to the original (and to create the right 'feel') the refrain has to begin and end with the same word, but with slightly different emphasis. Fortunately, 'rejoice' works well.

Gaudete! gaudete!
Christus est natus
ex Maria Virgine:
gaudete!

Tempus adest gratiae,
hoc quod optabamus;
carmina laeticiae
devote reddamus.

Deus homo factus est,
natura mirante;
mundus renovatus est
a Christo regnante.

Ezechielis porta
clausa pertransitur;
unde Lux est orta,
salus invenitur.

Ergo nostra concio
psallat jam in lustro;
benedicat Domino:
salus Regi nostro.

Bible references: Colossians 1.15, Hebrews 1.2.

133.
Ring, bells of Bethlehem
An Epiphany carol, written to a traditional English melody at the request of
the music editor of *Carol Praise*. I cannot recall how much of the
traditional text—if any—has been retained. The music arrangement there
is by Norman Warren. The words invite the wise among us to emulate the
magi who followed the star and presented their treasures to the young
child. So we too must welcome our king.

Bible references: Isaiah 60.3, Matthew 2.1

134.
Ring out the bells and let the people know
During my time as Rector of Eversley we reinstated the tower bells, which
had been silent for many years. I decided to write a hymn for the occasion,
and gained my inspiration from Bill Ind, who subsequently became Bishop
of Grantham. Bill and my wife Beatrice worked together assisting the
Bishop of Winchester with the care of ordinands. At the time in question,
Bill expressed a controversial (as far as I was concerned) opinion that
evangelizing the community did not matter so much as being the presence
of Christ there. In this view, poor numbers at church are insignificant; more
important is that the community knows someone is praying. So the church
bell should always be rung at times of prayer.

I felt that there was at least a half truth here; letting the people know we
are praying for them is a good step towards a more overtly evangelistic
initiative at a later date! Hence, stanza 1:
   To all around this truth the bells declare—
   'Your needs are lifted up to God in prayer!'

The hymn was first published in *The Ringing World*, the national magazine
of British change ringers. It is used most often to the tune *Wooodlands*.

Bible references: Exodus 28.35,   John 6.35,   John 6.51,   James 1.17,
Revelation 1.7.

135.
Ring out the bells, the joyful news is breaking
Past three a clock (spelling correct as here!) was the traditional English
carol tune to which these words were written.
   "Past three a clock, and a cold frosty morning;
   past three a clock: Good morrow, masters all!"

Once again, the received text is not one which lends itself to use in
worship; but the tune is fairly well known, and invites the creation of a
Christian carol.

A networked televised service from my church in Tonbridge in 1994 ended
with this carol. The cameras cut back and forth between the choir and
congregation in the church and the ringing loft in the tower. An error in the

mixing unit led to our excellent peal of bells being scarcely audible. The choir were satisfied, but not the bell-ringers.

I hope this text and melody will one day be arranged for hand-bell ringers.

Bible references: Genesis 1.3, 2 Chronicles 2.6, Matthew 28.6, Mark 16.6, Luke 2.20, Luke 24.3, John 20.2, Acts 2.1.

136.
Roar the waves
Written in 1978 at Bitterne. It's not for me to say but . . . This hymn is remarkable for its internal rhyming and structure, if nothing else! The primordial feel is intended to reflect the glory of God in creation, which, in the last stanza, is echoed by the church. It has Trinitarian stanza structure: Father, Son, Spirit. Stanza 1 was suggested by the *Psalms*, stanza 2 by 'Morning has broken', stanza 3 by a Roman Catholic song published in 1965 by the Medical Mission Sisters of Philadelphia 'Spirit of God in the clear running water', stanza 4 by a huge banner created by the Dominican sisters of the Vita et Pax community, then in Cockfosters, which was used as a backdrop for many renewal conferences in the UK.

The lighter side is the story that when *Roar the waves* was first published in *Hymns for Today's Church* it was indexed as '*Roar the wives*'. The editors' wives, who had much to endure during the compilation of that volume, viewed the misprint as entirely justifiable!

Genesis 1.20, Job 41.1, Psalm 21.13, Psalm 74.14, Psalm 78.4, Psalm 93.1, Psalm 104.26, Psalm 104.29, Isaiah 27.1, Daniel 7.13, Matthew 16.28, Matthew 24.30, Mark 13.26, Luke 21.27, John 3.8, Acts 17.25, Ephesians 5.19, Ephesians 6.18, Colossians 3.16, Hebrews 1.2, 1 John 1.2.

137.
Safe in the hands of God who made me
This text based on *Psalm 27* was written for *Psalm Praise*, but later modified for *Psalms for Today*. In stanza 3, *Psalm 27*.10 gave me the opportunity to express the gender inclusiveness of God, which was then becoming a hot issue: "Though my father and my mother forsake me, the Lord will take me into his care."

Bible reference: Psalm 27.

138.
Save me, O God, hear my prayer
Psalm 54 is short, and has problematic phrasing for use in Christian worship; viz. "I look with delight on the downfall of my enemies". Other writers I approached were disinclined, so the editor hauled in the slack once more. I aimed at a simple, short, straightforward text.

Bible reference: Psalm 54.

139.
Savior Christ, in mercy come
Savior of the World is a free church hymn from the 19th century, but of otherwise unknown origin. The editors of the Church of England's *Alternative Service Book 1980* decided to include it as the final canticle at Evening Prayer—hence our interest in including a version in *Psalms for Today*, which was designed especially to appeal to Anglicans.

This text I prepared jointly with my writer friend, David Mowbray. He worked the first draft and sent it to me for consideration. By the time I had finished making suggestions for improvement, it was scarcely recognizable. Since I have a great respect for his talent, it was with some confusion of face that I called him, and asked for permission to be radical. Graciously he accepted, and agreed upon the remolding of the text; hence we now share the copyright.

Bible references: John 10.11, John 16.12, John 17.21, Revelation 1.5.

140.
See him lying on a bed of straw (*Calypso Carol*)
Calypso Carol was written when I was a theological student—during my time at Oak Hill College in North London. There was a tradition of writing a carol to bring to a close the College Christmas Concert, and it was agreed that I should write and perform a new carol of my own making at the Concert in 1964. Present on the occasion were students and tutors who were to gain prominence in the Church of England, including my doctrine tutor, later to be Archbishop of Canterbury, George Carey.

The inspiration for *Calypso* came earlier, from a chance remark—and a fairly artless one—by Peter Hancock, then curate at Christ Church Beckenham. In a Christmas address to young people, he asked, "How would *you* like to be born in a stable?". Hence, "See him lying on a bed of straw etc."

In fact, *Calypso Carol* owes its popularity in England to a technical accident. A luckless BBC engineer wiped out the tape of the Kings College Cambridge Carol Service in the days before it went out 'live'. This event was a national tradition, and listening to it was part of many people's Christmas. The BBC hastily rearranged a service of carols, using the singer Cliff Richard (a household name in England, though scarcely known in the USA) as a draw. He chose to sing, among other items *Calypso Carol*, which then quickly became a 'standard' carol in the UK, and British Commonwealth countries. Indeed, it is sometimes difficult convincing broadcasters that it is not 'public domain'. I heard it announced on BBC Radio as 'that traditional folk carol from the West Indies'!

In 1983 the State of Nevis asked an English designer, Jennifer Toombs, to prepare a set of Christmas stamps. She chose *Calypso Carol* as her theme for illustration, and a set of four stamps were produced one value for each stanza of the carol: 5 cents, 'See him lying on a bed of straw'; 30 cents, 'Star of silver, sweep across the skies'; 55 cents, 'Angels, sing again the song you sang'; and $3, 'Mine are riches, from your poverty'.

Calypso Carol has been translated into German and Nordic languages. Only very recently has it begun to be published in North America. This was also one of my rare tunes—and by far the most successful. The original harmonization was done by Stephen Coates. A wide variety of other arrangements have found their way onto the market. There are many arrangements for children, a cathedral anthem setting made by John Bertalot before he moved to the Princeton and, most recently, a setting created for *Hope Publishing Company* by Alan Pote.

This carol—which now seems to me fairly artless—was in fact the beginning of my serious hymn writing; without it this book would not exist.

Bible references: Micah 5.2,   Matthew 2.1,   Matthew 2.11,   Luke 2.1, Luke 2.7,   Luke 2.7,   Luke 2.12,   Luke 2.13,   Luke 2.15,   Luke 2.16, John 3.16, John 4.42, Romans 11.33, 1 Corinthians 1.21, 2 Corinthians 8.9, 2 Corinthians 8.9,   2 Corinthians 8.9,   Ephesians 1.7,   Ephesians 1.11, Ephesians 3.3, Colossians 1.27, Titus 3.7, 1 John 4.14, 1 John 5.11.

141.
Shepherds, wake to news of joy
Written at Norman Warren's request for his music in the dance operetta *Welcome Your King!*

Bible reference: Luke 2.8.

142.
Shout aloud, girls and boys
Here is one of the translations of Latin carols that I did for *Carols for Today*. The original four stanzas were from *Piae Cantiones* (1582). The music, too, mediaeval; the previously popular arrangement by Gustav Holst (1874-1934).

Personent hodie	Magi tres venerunt,
Voces puerulae,	Parvulum inquirunt,
Laudantes jucundè	parvulum inquirunt,
Qui nobis est natus,	Stellulam sequendo,
Summo Deo datus,	Ipsum adorando,
Et de virgineo ventre procreatus.	Aurum, thus, et myrrham ei
	offerendo.
In mundo nascitur,	
Pannis involvitur,	Omnes clericuli,
Praesepi ponitur,	Pariter pueri,
Stabulo brutorum,	Cantent ut angeli:
Rector supernorum.	Advenisti mundo,
Perdidit spolia princeps	Laudes, tibi fundo.
infernorum.	Ideo gloria in excelsis Deo!

Of the various discussions about the English text, I remember one as to whether it was wise to invite "girls and boys" to "shout"; and another as to how we might separate the Epiphany visit of the magi from the Christmas story of the manger. Hence stanza 3.

Bible references: Matthew 1.23, Matthew 2.11.

143.

Silver star shining out over Bethlehem

During my schooldays at Dulwich I played percussion and timpani in the school orchestra. Annually we would perform at the *Royal Festival Hall* in London. On one memorable occasion at the dress rehearsal in the concert hall I missed one of those pivotal drum beats which come in the movement of Borodin's *Polovtsian Dance*. The whole orchestra, tense, poised and waiting for the mighty cue which never came, collapsed in mirth and the rehearsal was adjourned for everyone to recover. I was dared not to fail at the performance in front of thousands!

This experience seared into my mind the beginning of that movement and the ensuing melody. I was aware that the song *Stranger in Paradise* had been popular to the tune, but thought it sufficiently in the past not to be a problem to the reception of carol words. It was the first line "Silver star shining . . (which I took from my *Calypso Carol*: "Star of silver, sweep across the skies) that convinced me the idea was a good one.

The task was enjoyable, if not particularly easy. I fought to keep the atmospherics: "Holy night for a pilgrim to journey through", "Silent sky, full of wonder and mystery". I introduced some psalmic references, "splendor of God most high", "mantle of majesty"; and I made one or two allusions to past uses of the melody: "O give praise to the mighty Lord" (as in 'Khan Khon Chak'), and "the gate way of paradise" (as in *Stranger in Paradise*). The enterprise was risky, but after some years of publication and use I am satisfied that it works well.

Bible reference: Matthew 2.10.

144.

Sing to the Lord with a song

Jubilate member Noël Tredinnick has led the Langham Arts enterprise for some years. Their flagship is *Prom Praise*, the regular event when Noël conducts the *All Souls Orchestra* in their large Christian concerts at the Royal Albert Hall in London, the Royal Festival Hall, The Barbican Concert Hall, and elsewhere. Noël and the orchestra have performed frequently in the UK, and also far away from home—for instance in Moscow—always with great skill and to warm acclaim. Often they will amuse and delight with a 'fun' classical piece, and it was in this spirit that I promised Noël a psalm version based on Schubert's (1797-1828) *Marche Militaire (number 1)*. Hence, *Sing to the Lord*. The words have to be sung fairly quickly, and the *All Souls Orchestra* and choir have since used the text several times, to the amusement of breathless audiences.

The psalm celebrates the majesty and the power of God, which leads to exultation among worshippers.

Bible reference: Psalm 96.

145.
Sleep, Lord Jesus
Our declared policy for the carol books *Carols for Today* and *Carol Praise* was to make the carol texts as clearly intelligible to regular and visiting worshippers alike as was possible within the constraints of theology and good poetry. Hence, when we discovered that one of our colleagues, the able musician and choir director Tom Cunningham, had set these Latin words so beautifully, we decided that a new English version was a must.

> Dormi, Jesu! Mater ridet
> Quae tam dulcem somnum videt,
> Dormi, Jesu! blandule!
> Si non dormis, mater plorat
> Inter fila cantans orat,
> Blande, veni, somnule.

Samuel Taylor Coleridge is said to have discovered this text in a German village, copying them from a print and rendering them in English:

> Sleep, sweet babe! my cares beguiling
> Mother sits beside thee smiling;
> Sleep my darling tenderly!
> If thou sleep not, mother mourneth,
> singing as her wheel she turneth:
> Come, soft slumber, balmily!

. . . which explains why most users stick to the Latin! *Sleep, Lord Jesus* has obvious echoes of the original, but tries to be more than a straight lullaby. It alludes in particular to three Scripture texts: "Mary treasured up all these thing in her heart" (Luke 2.19), Simeon's comment to Mary, "This child is destined to be a sign that will be rejected; and you too will be pierced to the heart" (Luke 2.35), and "Meanwhile, near the cross on which Jesus was hung, his mother was standing" (John 19.25)

In terms of excellence, I yield everything to Tom's melody and arrangement; I trust that in time it will become universally known among choir directors seeking material for Christmas.

Bible references: Luke 2.7, Luke 2.19, Luke 2.35, John 19.25

146.
Soldiers marching
It was decided that a clearer Christmas narrative might be applied to the tune *Carol of the Drum*. Permission was obtained from *Columbia Pictures*

inc. to publish this text, and I was able to retain the words copyright for *Jubilate Hymns,* and *Hope Publishing Company.*

The strange 'marching' quality of the tune gave me the idea of setting the story of the massacre of the infants. Apart from the *Coventry Carol,* there is very little that treats this theme. I constructed the text so that the music could get louder as the soldiers approached Bethlehem in stanza 1, and softer as they marched away in stanza 3, their terrible deed completed.

There is a play of irony in this carol: in stanza 1 "for Herod's peace of mind" is matched in stanza 2 by "paying well to know where they are", and stanza 3 by "to Herod telling lies" (the implication there being that the soldiers would have told Herod that their mission was completed).

Bible reference: Matthew 2.16.

147.
Songs of gladness, songs of gladness
This is without apology a simple round set to *Frère Jacques* for simple circumstances (a Christmas service with children present). I put it here because it is useful rather than worthy; there is nothing at all profound—I won't even attempt Bible references!

Bible reference: Luke 2.10.

148.
Sovereign Lord, in all the earth
This was very early attempt at a *Psalm 8* version; again, not profound, but a good tune could lift it. It has the merit of staying with the psalm's verbs—singular and plural. And it is all too easy to be heavy-handed with *Psalm 8,* detracting from the individual testimony of the diminutive psalmist as he gazes out at the vastness of space.

Bible reference: Psalm 8.

149.
Surely God the Lord is good
Psalm 73 is true to many a Christian's experience; we nearly lose our foothold when we see the prosperity of those who do not honor God. "Surely in vain I have kept my heart pure" (*Psalm 73.13*). Out of this depression is rekindled the flame of faith, and of love for God: "Whom have I in heaven but you?"

  'When my stumbling footsteps tire,
strengthen me in all I do—
earth has no more I desire;
whom have I in heaven but you?

'This earth-bound fantasy shall disperse when you arise': the allusion of the third stanza is to the hot sun which, rising, disperses the dreamy quality of the morning mist and all its illusions; eventually the pure blue sky becomes visible.

Bible reference: Psalm 73.

150.
The brightness of God's glory
Written on a campsite at Hayle, Cornwall, in 1980; by intention, a paraphrase of *Hebrews* 1 and a statement of Christology. The vacation was dreadful from the point of view of the weather and the cramped conditions; for some reason we had taken—most unusually—three weeks' leave. But the writing of this and other hymns just flowed. It may have been something to do with the wind and the bracing air.

Bible references: 2 Corinthians 4.4,   Colossians 1.15,   Hebrews 1, Hebrews 7.16.

151.
The God of heaven thunders
This was my first attempt to break away from a rigid representation of a psalm text, and to appeal instead to the wonderful imagery which we find in these nature psalms. I wrote it in approximately 1971, at a time when we were scarcely conscious of the exclusive language issue with regard to 'men', let alone in respect of God. And I suppose I was a little more adventurous with unusual words. It was published first in *Psalm Praise*. The text then read:

> The God of heaven thunders;
> *his* voice in cadent echoes
> resounds above the waters—
> and all the world sings,
>   Glory, glory, glory!

> The desert writhes in tempest,
> wind whips the trees to fury,
> *sear* lightning splits the forest
> and flame diffuses
>   glory, glory, glory.

> The mighty God eternal
> is to *his* throne ascended,
> and we who are *his* people
> within these walls cry,
>   Glory, glory, glory!

The original text was revised in deference to English conservatism and American correctness—but I would be delighted to see it published again in its early form.

Bible reference: Psalm 29.

152.

The hands of Christ
During the period 1965-1968 I served my title (did my apprenticeship) at
St. Helen's Parish Church in Lancashire. I confess to an impatience with
my vicar's preaching, and resorted to writing prayers or articles on the
subject of his sermon. On one occasion I had pen and paper poised, but was
quite unable to do anything but listen! He was preaching upon the head,
hands, feet and side of the crucified Jesus. The sequence impressed itself
upon me and, years later, I did take pen to paper to write this hymn.

I feel it is my best. It is unconcentional in form, although regular in meter
until the last line. It employs various devices for emphasis: note in
particular the reversal within the first line of each stanza, and the build up
of tension towards the end of each. And it is not afraid to innovate:

" . . they ringed his head with briars woven"
" . . they mocked (his lips) with wine" etc.

It combines shock at what the religious leaders did to Jesus with a careful
sarcasm about their twisted principles:

"for sacrilege they could not bear—
the Sabbath comes, so they must tear
    the heart from God."

This hymn is also one of the only three for which I feel I have written a
satisfying melody. (There's always another one on the way!) It was floating
around in my mind for about ten years, but I could never capture it (until it
resolved in the bath in 1992!). I called the tune *Beatrice* after my long-
suffering wife who has put up with—even encouraged—my writing
addiction.

Bible references: Psalm 22.16,   Zechariah 12.10,   Matthew 27.29,
Matthew 27.34,   Matthew 27.35,   Matthew 27.48,   Matthew 28.6,
Mark 15.14,   Mark 15.17,   Mark 15.23,   Mark 15.36,   Mark 16.6,
Luke 13.22, Luke 23.33, Luke 23.36, Luke 24.6, John 14.6, John 19.2,
John 19.18, John 19.29, John 19.31, John 19.34, John 19.37, John 20.25,
Romans 5.1, 1 Corinthians 2.8, 1 Peter 2.24.

153.

The majesty of mountains
After the second world war, the theologian and Old Testament scholar
Gerhard Von Rad was rewarded for his steadfast opposition to Nazism, and
his world-wide academic reputation by a gift of land at Endorf in the
foothills of the Bavarian Alps. After his death, his son Ulrich and his
daughter-in-law Annemarie had a chalet house erected on part of this land.
I had known and befriended Annemarie as a child and a student. In the
early days of my ministry Ulrich and Annemarie helped me to lead two
large youth conferences/house parties in Bavaria. By this time I was
married, and so the friendship between the families was cemented. On the
first occasion when we visited the younger Von Rads in their Bavarian

home we stayed on in their absence and enjoyed the staggeringly beautiful countryside. The view of the Alps from the balcony of the chalet was spectacular and breathtaking. I wrote a poem by way of thanks to them—and it grew into a hymn.

David Iliff, my music editor for *Psalms for Today* felt that the alliteration was quite 'over the top', but sent it to John Barnard for a second opinion. John confesses he did not even notice the alliteration and promptly wrote a tune. On this basis, we included it in the book.

Bible reference: Psalm 104.

154.
The story has broken
Once again, a traditional English melody—*The Ash Grove*—was there, inviting carol words. We sensed another opportunity to provide familiar music with lyrics which would enable use in a worship service at a time of year when many casual visitors attend our UK churches. The words were published in *Carol Praise*. The greatest difficulty in creating this carol was to find sufficient matching pairs of syllables for so many rhymes in such a short compass—and still make sense!

Bible reference: Luke 2.10.

155.
There's a bright sky over Bethlehem
As far as I can recall, this carol began as a translation/paraphrase of a Danish Carol sent to me by Ester Jensen of Kibaek, Jutland. Ester is a Roman Catholic and a teacher of English; she collected favorite Danish carols for us when she knew of the *Jubilate* carol book projects. The original tune is in my mind, but I cannot find it in any of our books—though the words are there. Roger Mayor, who led the choirs for the last Billy Graham London crusades, has written the tune *Marloes*.

Bible reference: Luke 2.13.

156.
To God's loving-kindness
Dr. Alan Oakley John and his wife Gene (Genevieve) were to depart for Southern Sudan as missionaries. Alan was the senior partner in his group of six doctors in general practice. Just as he had reached the top, so to speak, he decided to train with the Anglican *Church Missionary Society*. Gene, who had been born in China of missionary parents, enjoyed the challenge, trained with him and served with him. I wrote this song in 1982 specifically for their farewell service. It was subsequently published in *Jesus Praise* and *Church Family Worship*.

Bible reference: Numbers 6.24.

157.
To lead a blameless life, O Lord
Once again, here is a most difficult psalm to versify for use in any Christian sense. In *Psalm 26* the psalmist protests his blamelessness, godliness and his the superior morality. The principles are worthy—but it's for someone else to say! I puzzled as to how these good principles might be expressed for the worshipper. There were two possibilities that I could see. One was the 'if . .' of Rudyard Kipling ("If I lead a blameless life . . ." etc.)—but I had used that elsewhere, in *If we love the word of God*. The other was a statement of principle—the form I eventually adopted—finishing with a prayer: "Let this be my supreme desire . . ." etc.

Michael Dawney, who wrote the first tune to this hymn, died at a young age in 1994.

Bible reference: Psalm 26.

158.
To those who rule our land
While the sentiments of *Psalm 72* are contemporary, the immediate reference is to the omnipotent Hebrew king. In order to be useful in contemporary worship, even in a constitutional monarchy, the allusions have to be wider than this. Hence this hymn version of the psalm petitions God not just for "the king", but for "those who rule our land"

Bible reference: Psalm 72.

159.
To your praise, O God almighty
To the praise of God the Father was first published in 1973, set for All Saints tide in the new canticle section of *Psalm Praise*). The text was subsequently revised inclusively. It combines thoughts from *1 Chronicles 29* and *Revelation* chapters 4 and 5, to give an anthem of the saints of God, exalting the sovereignty of God and the worthiness of Christ.

Bible references: 1 Chronicles 29, Revelation 4, Revelation 5.

160.
We are a world divided
"You have rejected us, O God, and burst forth upon us . . you have shaken the land and torn it open: mend its fractures, for it is quaking" (*Psalm 60*.1,2)

Originally the hymn began 'We are a land divided', the emphasis reflecting the English churches' concerns about the "two nations" division of Britain, under rule and legislation that seemed to ignore the needs of the poor. This concern was central to our thinking when I was a member of the community affairs board of the *British Council of Churches*. It was expressed in the influential document *Faith in the City* (1985) published by the Church of England (which denomination we agreed "was in the best position to do it") but supported by the other churches. The evidence is that *Faith in the City* and its thinking substantially influenced the Thatcher government, despite their early 'rejection' of it. During this period, the whole church again learned to be 'prophetic' about issues of social justice.

Bible reference: Psalm 60.

161.
We give God thanks for those who knew
This was written in 1975 at Bitterne, to meet the need for a hymn for Christian Aid Week—a hymn which was an expression both of social concern and of spiritual intent. My thoughts were in particular for those who had no medical ability, nor were able to give significant financial help to the need of the suffering. 'Yet we still can help' is the message of the hymn. I was experimenting with deliberate 'inversions' at the time; and you will see this in the last line of each stanza.

Bible references: Jeremiah 30.17,   Matthew 8.2,   Matthew 8.3, Matthew 9.20, Matthew 15.31, Matthew 17.7, Matthew 20.34, Mark 1.40, Mark 1.41,   Mark 5.27,   Mark 6.56,   Mark 7.33,   Mark 8.22,   Luke 4.18, Luke 4.40,   Luke 5.12,   Luke 5.13,   Luke 8.44,   Luke 10.34, 1 Corinthians 12.9,   1 Corinthians 16.2,   Ephesians 6.18,   Colossians 4.3, 1 Thessalonians 5.25, 2 Thessalonians 3.1, Hebrews 13.18.

162.
We hail the approaching God
This advent carol is based on the Latin text below by Charles Coffin (1676-1749), Rector of the University of Paris. It was published in 1736 in Coffin's *Hymni Sacri*, and included in the *Paris Breviary* for that year—for Matins in advent. The hymn *The advent of our King* was based on the translation by J Chandler (1806-1876).

Instantis adventum Dei
poscamus ardenti prece
festique munus inclytum
praeoccupemus canticis.

aeterna proles feminae
non horret includi sinu;
fit ipse servus, ut jugo
nos servitutis eximat.

mansuetus et clemens venit;
occurre, festina Sion:
ultro tibi quam porrigit,
ne dura pacem respuas.

mox nube clara fulgurans

mundi redibit arbiter,
suique membra corporis
caelo triumphator vehet.

fetus tenebrarum, die
cedant propinquo crimina;
Adam reformetur vetus,
imago succedat novi.

qui liberator advenis,
Fili, tibi laus maxima
cum Patre et almo Spiritu
in sempiterna saecula.

Bible references: Daniel 7.13, Zechariah 9.9, Matthew 24.30, Mark 13.26, Mark 14.62, Revelation 22.20.

163.

We have heard, O Lord our God

Psalm 44 is a song of remembrance which declares that it is the Lord who gives the victory. In a church which is, rightly, wary of triumphalism, the interpretation has to be one of thanksgiving and looking to the future. With the psalmist we confess how little we appreciate the favor of the Lord. So much so that, despite all God has done for us, we have allowed shameful things to happen in our society. The hymn was written for, and published in, *Psalms for Today.*

Bible reference: Psalm 44.

164.

We lift our hearts up to the Lord

This strange text—more poem than hymn—was first written in the singular 'I lift my heart up to the Lord' for the *Hymns for Today's Church* committee but not selected for the book. *We lift our hearts up to the Lord* starts from no particular scripture, more from a sense of security in God despite present foreboding. My seminary days were during the Cuban missile crisis, through to the assassination of President John F Kennedy; morality was in decline, theology was in despair. I went to see Ibsen. Looking back on it, we grew up suddenly, and some of the experiences were painful and left scars. Hence stanzas 2 and 3. The final stanza, with its dark skies, empty trees and shrill cries is not just the winter of life, but the nuclear shadow. Yet God is there, at the end as at the beginning.

Bible references: Job 19.8, Psalm 6.9, Psalm 8.35, Psalm 18.6, Psalm 28.6, Psalm 35.9, Psalm 40.1, Psalm 66.19, Psalm 116.1, Isaiah 25.9, Philippians 3.8, Philippians 4.7.

165.

We share a new day's dawn

This is the Christian's resolution in the early morning—to live the new day for Christ. It was written in 1981 at West Lakes, near Whitehaven in Cumbria. Note the repetitive construction: 'Christ' comes consistently in the first two lines of each stanza, and 'serve' or 'service' in each third line. Again, in each stanza the third line picks up a key word from the first line, and the fourth line takes up the theme and wording of the first line. No one was more surprised than I when in 1994, the BBC Television *Songs of Praise* program decided to have *We share a new day's dawn* sung (adapted) from the Covent Garden Piazza in London to the melody of Nessum Dorma ('none shall sleep tonight')!

Bible references: Psalm 111.9, 1 John 4.18.

166.

We thank you, God for feeding us

276

This is the only surviving text of a group devised to match the prayers of the Church of England's *Alternative Service Book 1980*—in this case, the thanksgiving collect after Communion.

Almighty God,
we thank you for feeding us
with the body and blood of your Son Jesus Christ.
Through him we offer you
our souls and bodies
to be a living sacrifice.
Send us out in the power of your Spirit
to live and work
to your praise and glory. **Amen.**

The prayer reflects the first of the two Thanksgivings which followed the Eucharistic Prayer in the 1662 *Book of Common Prayer*. The same allusion to *Romans* 12.1, will be noted.

Bible references: Matthew 26.26, Matthew 28.19, Mark 14.22, Mark 16.15, Luke 22.19, Luke 24.49, John 6.63, Acts 18, Romans 12.1, Romans 15.19, 1 Corinthians 11.24, Ephesians 3.16, 2 Timothy 1.7.

167.
We will tell each generation
"What we have heard and known,
what our fathers have told us,
we will not hide it from our children;
we will tell the next generation" (*Psalm 78*.3,4)

Psalm 78 begins to tell the history of the Hebrews under the hand of God—of their adventure and their rebellion, of God's blessing and God's punishment. This is a cautionary tale developed as worship. I have tried in this hymn text to apply the same principle to our own nation's history. But the experience of threat and deliverance is common enough, and I hope the sentiments are universal, so that the hymn can be used elsewhere.

Central to the psalm is the relating of the manna episode, God's provision despite the people's petulance.
"He rained down manna for the people to eat." (*Psalm 78*.24)

I was therefore able to focus in on both eucharist and absolution for the concluding stanza:
Tell the grace that falls from heaven,
angels' food as faith's reward;
tell how sins may be forgiven
through the mercy of the Lord.

Bible reference: Psalm 78.

168.

Welcome, Child of Mary

Welcome, Child of Mary was based on a translation from the Dutch (*Nu zijt wellekome*) at the time of preparation of *Carols for Today* and *Carol Praise*.

Nu zijt wellekome
Jezu lieve Heer.
Gij komt van al zo hoge
Van al zo veer.
Nu zijt wellekome van de hoge hen
Hier al op dit aardrijk zijt gij gezien nooit meer:
Kyrielys.

Herders op de velden
hoorden een nieuw lied.
Dat Jezus was geboren
Zij wisten 't niet.
Gaat aan gene straten en gij zult hem vinden klaar,
Bethl'hem is de stede daar is 't geschiedt voorwaar:
Kyrielys.

Wijzen uit het Oosten
Uit zo verre land
Zij zochten onze Here
met offerand'.
Z'offerden ootmoedelijk, mirr' wierook ende goud,
Ter ere van dit kinde dat alle ding behoudt:
Kyrielys.

Paul Wigmore and I attempted the paraphrase simultaneously; eventually, his version was published in *Carols for Today*, and mine in *Carol Praise*—both to the same arrangement by John Barnard of the Dutch tune.

Bible references: Matthew 2.11, Luke 2.11.

169.

Welcome, Jesus Child of Mary

Written to the German carol tune *O du fröhliche* in the absence of any pleasing modern translation. My attempt is far from profound; I include it for the sake of completeness, but would gladly bury it in favor of a better!

Bible references: Matthew 2.2,   Matthew 12.23,   Matthew 21.9, Romans 5.4, 2 Peter 1.19, Revelation 1.7.

170.

Welcome, welcome, Savior come to Bethlehem

Written for Norman Warren's Christmas dance operetta, 'Welcome Your King', this song celebrates the arrival of the humble Lord of heaven "among the poor".

Bible references:
171.

When God from heaven to earth came down

278

Like many folk carols, *I saw three ships* is now obscure in its allusion and remote from the purpose of Christian worship. Nevertheless, the tune lives on in popular consciousness, and therefore makes an excellent vehicle for Christmas words that *can* be used in church services; especially services which attract the casual visitor, as do so many carol services in the UK.

When God from heaven has proved to be a useful resource for Christmas Day services, not least for occasions when children are present. The repeated "on Christmas day, on Christmas Day" enables participation even by those who cannot read. Stanzas 1 to 3 tell the familiar story, and stanza 4 picks up on traditional phrases of Christmas celebration as a climax to the carol—so linking the new words with the ethos of the melody. At least, that is the intention!

Bible reference: Luke 2.20.

172.
When I lift up my voice (You are my refuge)
At the time of preparing texts for *Psalms for Today* and *Songs from the Psalms* traditional hymn writers in the UK were beginning to see their genre being swiftly overtaken by the contemporary song idiom. On reflection, this has happened for two reasons: first, there is the demise of four part choirs and organs in many churches, along with the rise of band accompaniment. This has meant that texts bound to melodies allied to traditional accompaniment have been deserted. The other reason is that, on the whole, song-writers devise their own texts. Indeed, they are aware that if they don't they may lose their copyright to the author of the text they set. While this means that musicians are at last getting the profile they have always deserved, it also means that the work of many of our authors is in cold storage.

In order to redress the situation, some of us who specialize in words have tried writing in a free-er song style. This representation of *Psalm 142* is an example. But, of course, everything then depends on the music—which is normally out of our control.

Bible reference: Psalm 142.

173.
When I'm afraid, I will trust in God
"When I'm afraid I will trust in you, in God, whose word I praise; in God I will trust, I will not be afraid, what can anyone do to me?" (*Psalm 56*.3, 4)

This is an intentionally poetic representation of the psalm—yet it fastens on to verses 3 and 4, because much that surrounds them will not be the current situation of most members of a church congregation. The psalm begins,

"The enemy assail me—all day long they press their attack".

A device which can be used to make this sort of text relevant to current worshippers is the conditional, "When . . ."—viz. "When the enemy attacks me . . ." Having spotted the conditional phrasing of the original psalm's verses 3 and 4 above, I began the stanzas of my poem:

"When I'm afraid . . ."
"When I'm alone . . ."
"While I'm alive . . ."

. . . asking: "In the light of my relationship with God, how can real harm come to me?" Which is the recurrent theme of the psalm.

Bible reference: Psalm 56.

174.
When Jesus Christ was eight days old

Geoffrey Dearmer (1867–1936) wrote *When Jesus Christ was yet a child he had a garden small*, based on a translation from a Plechtchéev text—to music by Peter Ilich Tchaikovsky (1840-1893). A worthy Victorian peace, but not a vehicle for Elizabethan praise. Hence the proposed *When Jesus Christ was eight days old*. This text represents the presentation of Jesus in the Temple, and the discovery by the aged Simeon of the light to lighten the world.

Bible reference: Luke 2.22.

175.
When Jesus walked upon this earth

When Jesus walked upon this earth was written in 1981 at West Lakes, near Whitehaven in Cumbria, an area later notorious because of the claimed contamination from nuclear power station out-fall on the beach. The *Jubilate* team invited various authors inside and outside their company to attempt a hymn about Jesus' earthly life. I observe that the text illustrates my 1980 fascination with repeated phrases, and elaborates the previous interest of my Passion tide hymns in the physical attributes of Jesus—now becoming abstract in 'word', 'touch', 'heart', 'name'. Each last line picks up the thought of each confronting second line. Stanza four, line two originally read, 'his name was 'king'' to match the other second lines. However, the *Hymns for Today's Church* editors would not pass that (since they knew various people whose name was 'King'!). I did think that 'his name was God' might do; with a consequent 'witness to his Godly name' in the last line.

Bible reference: Psalm 107.10, Isaiah 42.7, Isaiah 61.1, Matthew 8.28, Matthew 10.1, Matthew 12.28, Matthew 20.28, Mark 3.27, Mark 10.45, Luke 4.18, Luke 6.17, Luke 9.1, Luke 11.20, Luke 22.26, 1 John 3.8

176.

When my bitter foes surround

Psalm 43 conveys personal sentiments about oppression and persecution—which is not continually the situation of worshippers, and rarely of a whole congregation simultaneously. It does not make much sense, then, to represent the *Psalm 37* as it is. Nevertheless, we all face troubles at some time—and this is when we feel most dependent on God's merciful protection and help, so the psalm does indeed have a relevance. But how to turn it into a hymn? Once again the conditional tense is employed: "When my bitter foes surround", "When deep sorrows overpower" etc.

Bible reference: Psalm 43.

177.

When shepherds watched and angels sang

At the time of writing I had either forgotten or overlooked the W. D. Dix (1837-1898) carol *What child is this*. This oversight led to my writing a new carol to the traditional English melody (before 1642) *Greensleeves*.

In order to placate publishers, we were trying to make a clear difference between our two books *Carols for Today* (Hodder & Stoughton) and *Carol Praise* (HarperCollins). So we put the Dix words in *Carols for Today*, the book with the more traditional music arrangements, and the Perry words in *Carol Praise*, the altogether lighter volume.

I must say I admire the Dix version, which achieves more internal rhyming than mine. The present text, however, is usefully narrative, and so suitable for a situation with children present.

Bible reference: Luke 2.8.

178.

When the angel came to Mary

My English text was written to utilise the traditional Cornish melody of the *Sans Day Carol*. The carol was so named because the traditional first three verses and the melody were taken down at St. Day in the parish of Gwennap, Cornwall. The *Oxford Book of Carols* recalls that St. Day, or St They was a saint from Brittany in France. The first line was in English:
   Now the holly bears a berry as white as the milk
And in Cornish:
   Mar gron war'n gelinen

Bible reference: Luke 1.26

179.

When the waters cover me (When my sorrows cover me)

The first musician to set this text was David Llewellyn Green. His music was published in *Come, Rejoice!*, a *Jubilate* hymn sampler prepared for me to take to the USA for the 1989 *Hymn Society* conference which was in Grand Rapids that year. I was able to demonstrate several of the works by *Jubilate* members, with the help of Sue (Mitchell) Wallace who kindly sight-read them for me, using the recently installed Calvin College chapel organ. Of all the material, the arrangement of this melody drew the most amusing (to an Englishman) comments from musicians in the assembled company: "Oh, the chromatics, the chromatics!" And truly, the music is a tour de force. It also created a considerable impression at the launch of *Psalms for Today* in Westminster Abbey the following year (1990). My hope is that the David Llewellyn Green arrangement will emerge in a fully choral version at a later stage in the USA.

The hymn is also published in a variant text *When my sorrows cover me*. Somehow, Chris Rolinson who wrote a song-style tune had already recorded and published a draft text before the editors had noticed he had the wrong one!

When my sorrows cover me,
   save me, O God;
when my friends abandon me,
when I seek what cannot be,
when I look and cannot see,
   (save me, O God,)
   save me, O God.
	You know all my guilty fears,
	   thank you, O God;
	you have heard with open ears,
	you have seen my contrite tears,
	you will bless my future years,
	   (thank you, O God,
	   thank you, O God,)
	   thank you, O God.

Bible reference: Psalm 69.

180.
When we walk with God, we are blessed
Psalm 1 has obvious difficulties for the contemporary versifier; "Blessed is the man" is not an auspicious start in the context of the present inclusive language debate. Also, like many other psalms, the contrast between the righteous (too obviously 'us') and the wicked (quite definitely 'them') allows of no shades of gray. This time, the temporal conditional "when" is applied to overcome the exclusive "men":
"When we walk with God, we are blessed"

The intended scansion is "blessed" (=blest) not "bless-ed". It is surely wise to avoid "bless-ed" in contemporary hymns and liturgies, since the only surviving use of this two-syllable word outside Christian piety is in such unfortunate contexts as:
"He is a bless-ed nuisance." OR
"She is rather bless-ed."—meaning affecting super-piety.

Bible reference: Psalm 1.

181.

Who can bind the raging sea

God answers Job out of the storm *(Job 38)*
> "What is the way the abode of light . . ?"
> "Who cuts a channel for the torrents of rain . . ?"
> "Do you send the lightning bolts on their way . . ?"
> "Do you satisfy the hunger of the lion cubs . . ?"
> "Who provides food for the raven when its young cry out to God . . ?"
> "Do you know when the mountain goats give birth . . ?"

This evocative series of questions to Job come at the end of the narrative. They establish in the poem not only God's sovereignty, but his role in creation. This hymn is intended to celebrate both; I found the writing of it a wonderful exercise. In this case I wrote out of admiration for the passage, and not for any particular publication; as far as I am aware it is not yet published in a hymnal.

Bible references: Job 38, Job 39.

182.

Who is this child

There are echoes here, of course, of W C Dix's *What Child is this*, and I guess that I was influenced, at least subconsciously, by his example.

The purpose of writing was to bring into Christmas use the lyrical Irish folk-song *Londonderry Air*. At the time of writing I was chaplain to the national Police Staff College at Bramshill in Hampshire. Here senior officers were trained to command the police forces of England, Wales and Northern Ireland (there were also contingents from all parts of the world). At any dinner or celebration where music was played, there would always be the *Londonderry Air* "O Danny boy" sung for the encouragement of the Irish police whom, along with their families, were then daily subjected to bombs and bullets. All other members of the police service held them in high regard, and the singing of this Irish melody was the regular tribute to their bravery.

For me, the song came to have a great poignancy; so that when we decided to add it to the list of well-known melodies to which we would write carols I decided upon a text of bravery and tenderness:
> "Who is this child . . who spurns the night and braves the winter wild?
> Was ever babe so lowly and so tender,
> yet full of grace? Who is this little child?"

Bible reference: Colossians 1.15.

183.

You laid the foundations of earth

This hymn was prepared as a psalm version based on *Psalm 102*. But I also had in mind *Hebrews 1*, which quotes extensively from that psalm:

"In the beginning, O Lord,
you laid the foundations of earth,
and the heavens are the work of your hands.
They will perish, but you remain.
You will roll them up like a robe;
like a garment they will be changed,
but you remain the same
and your years will never end."

This passage from *Hebrews* is the Epistle set for Christmas Day in the 1662 *Book of Common Prayer* and so has impressed itself on the consciousness of every Anglican of my generation and before.

Bible References: Psalm 102, Hebrews 1.10

Bible Index of Hymns and Songs

125.1	God the Father of creation—57
130.5	O God beyond all praising—115
135.1	Angels, praise him—4
135.5	Come, worship God—29
136.	Give thanks to God, for he is good—41
136.26	Not the grandeur of the mountains—107
137.	Babylon, by the rivers of sorrow—6
137.	By flowing waters of Babylon—15
137.	By rivers of sorrow we sat—16
138.	I'll praise you, Lord—77
141.	O Lord, come quickly when I call—119
141.2	Now evening comes—108
142.	When I lift up my voice—172
144.2	God is our fortress and our rock—49, 50
147.8	Like a mighty river flowing—95
148.	Praise him, praise him, praise him—130
148.1	Angels, praise him—4
149, 150	Bring to the Lord a glad new song—14
150.1	Angels, praise him—4
150.6	Jesus Christ the Lord is born—85

Proverbs

18.24	Jesus, Redeemer, come—88

Ecclesiastes

12.13	O God beyond all praising—115

Song of Songs

8.6	O Jesus, my Lord—118

Isaiah

6.7	Jesus, Redeemer, come—88
6.8	How shall they hear—69
9.2	God whose love we cannot measure—58
9.2	In the darkness of the night—82
9.6	A child is born in Bethlehem—1
9.6	Come and hear the joyful singing—24
11.1	Bethlehem, the chosen city of our God—8
11.10	Jesus, hope of every nation—86
25.9	We lift our hearts up to the Lord—164
26.3	Like a mighty river flowing—95
26.3	Not the grandeur of the mountains—107
27.1	Roar the waves—136
33.11	Born of the water—13
33.11	I believe in God the Father—71
35.1	Let the desert sing—92
41.14	I believe in God the Father—71
41.14	Jesus, hope of every nation—86
41.18	Let the desert sing—92

Joel

2.1, 15, 31

        Blow upon the trumpet—11

Micah

5.2	Bethlehem, the chosen city of our God—8
5.2	Bethlehem, what greater city—9
5.2	Calypso Carol—140
5.2	Jesus Christ the Lord is born—85
5.2	See him lying on a bed of straw—140
7.8	God whose love we cannot measure—58
7.14	God our Father, bless your people—53

Habakkuk

3.17	God is our fortress and our rock—49, 50

Zechariah

9.9	We hail the approaching God—162
9.14	Blow upon the trumpet—11
12.10	The hands of Christ—152

Matthew

1.1	O bless the God of Israel—110
1.23	Shout aloud, girls and boys—142
2.1	Calypso Carol—140
2.1	Glory in the highest heaven—46
2.1	Jesus Christ the Lord is born—85
2.1	Ring, bells of Bethlehem—133
2.1	See him lying on a bed of straw—140
2.1	The shepherd guards his sheep—
2.2	Jesus Christ the Lord is born—85
2.2	Welcome, Jesus, Child of Mary—169
2.5	Bethlehem, what greater city—9
2.9	Journey to Bethlehem—91
2.10	Silver star—143
2.11	Calypso Carol—140
2.11	Come and praise the Lord our king—25
2.11	Come and sing the Christmas story—26
2.11	See him lying on a bed of straw—140
2.11	Shout aloud, girls and boys—142
2.11	Welcome, Child of Mary—168
2.13	Jesus Christ the Lord is born—85
2.16	Soldiers marching—146
2.18	Jesus Christ the Lord is born—85
3.11	Born of the water—13
3.11	I believe in God the Father—71
4.1	God save and bless our nation—54
4.15	Jesus, hope of every nation—86

293

John

Acts

299

Topical Index of Hymns and Songs

Abraham
47—Glory to the Lord of love (canticle)
126—O praise the Lord, the mighty God (canticle)

Advent
11—Blow upon the trumpet
32—Creator of the stars of light
59—God will arise (Psalm 12)
82—In the darkness of the night
86—Jesus, hope of every nation (canticle)
87—Jesus is our refuge (Psalm 46)
92—Let the desert sing
93—Lift up your hearts to the Lord (canticle)
103—Mary sang a song (canticle, Mary)
106—No sorrow, no mourning, no crying
110—O bless the God of Israel (canticle)
114—O come, our world's Redeemer
120—O Lord, my rock, to you I cry (Psalm 120)
121—O Lord, my rock, to you I cry (Variant) (Psalm 120)
126—O praise the Lord, the mighty God (canticle)
134—Ring out the bells and let the people
149—Surely God the Lord is good (Psalm 73)
162—We hail the approaching God
183—You laid the foundations of earth (Psalm 102)

Affirmation
56—God the Father caused to be
57—God the Father of creation
71—I believe in God the Father

animals
81—In majesty and splendor (Psalm 104)
181—Who can bind the raging sea

Annunciation
40—Gabriel the angel came
103—Mary sang a song (canticle)
178—When the angel came to Mary

answer
73—I love you, Lord, my rock (Psalm 18)

anxiety
124—O Lord, the God who saves me (Psalm 88)

Ascension
45—Glory be to God in heaven (canticle)

306

34—Fear not, for I bring all people (angels, Bethlehem, news)
37—From heaven above I come to bring (angels, humility, manger, news)
38—From highest heaven where praises ring (humility, news)
40—Gabriel the angel came (Gabriel, Mary, obedience)
43—Glad music fills the Christmas sky (angels, cross, lullaby, peace)
46—Glory in the highest heaven (angels, glory, shepherds, world)
61—Happy Christmas, everybody (greeting, morning, worship)
66—Hear the skies around (angels, gloria)
67—Here we come a-caroling (angels, peace, shepherds)
70—Hush, little baby (angels, Joseph, manger, Mary, shepherds)
78—In a stable, in a manger (child, manger, Mary, morning, sinners)
82—In the darkness of the night (angels, darkness, light, midnight)
84—Jesus, Child of Mary (angels, cross, humility, Mary, worship)
85—Jesus Christ the Lord is born (angels, bells, Herod, magi, shepherds)
90—Jesus, savior, holy child (birth, humble, lullaby, Mary, night, poor)
91—Journey to Bethlehem (magi)
94—Lift your heart and raise your voice (angels, gloria, humility, shepherds)
101—Lullaby, little Jesus (angels, lullaby, stable)
102—Mary and Joseph, praise with them (angels, creator, Joseph, Mary, shepherds)
103—Mary sang a song (canticle, Mary)
113—O come, Christians, wonder (child, love, poor, sin)
118—O Jesus, my Lord (angels, child, poor, poverty)
127—On a night when all the world (angels, magi, night, shepherds, stable)
132—Rejoice with heart and voice (creation, dedication, Mary)
133—Ring, bells of Bethlehem (bells, magi, star)
135—Ring out the bells, the joyful news (angels, bells, night, prophets, shepherds)
140—See him lying on a bed of straw (angels, cross, forgiveness, magi, manger, Mary, shepherds, sorrow, stable, star)
141—Shepherds, wake to news of joy (angel, midnight, poor, shepherds)
142—Shout aloud, girls and boys (choir, magi, Mary, peace, poor, stranger)
143—Silver star (heaven, humility, magi, night, poverty, star)
145—Sleep, Lord Jesus (child, Mary, redemption, sin)
146—Soldiers marching (Herod, magi)
147—Songs of gladness (bells)
154—The story has broken (angel, humility, shepherds)
155—There's a bright sky over Bethlehem (angels, magi, shepherds, stable, star)
168—Welcome, Child of Mary (angels, magi, Mary, shepherds)
169—Welcome, Jesus, Child of Mary (Mary)
170—Welcome, welcome, Savior (angels, glory, poor)

171—When God from heaven to earth came down (angels, incarnation, organ, shepherds)

177—When shepherds watched and angels sang (Christmas Day, Herod, Joseph, love, magi, Mary, shepherds)

178—When the angel came to Mary (angel, Mary)

182—Who is this child (Child, night, praise, witness, Word)

church

52—God of light and life's creation

106—No sorrow, no mourning, no crying

131—Praise the Father, God of justice

157—To lead a blameless life, O Lord (Psalm 26)

city

83—In the streets of every city

cleansing

36—Food to pilgrims given (communion)

63—Heal me, hands of Christ

64—Heal me, hands of Jesus

comfort

58—God whose love we cannot measure (prayer)

106—No sorrow, no mourning, no crying

117—O gracious Lord, be near me (Psalm 6)

Communion

3—All who are thirsty (refreshment)

5—As we walk along beside you (Easter, presence, word)

36—Food to pilgrims given (cleansing, feeding)

42—Given by grace (forgiveness, peace, release)

83—In the streets of every city (witness)

105—My faithful shepherd is the Lord (Psalm 23)

115—O God beyond all praising

134—Ring out the bells and let the people

149—Surely God the Lord is good (Psalm 73)

166—We thank you, God (dedication, witness)

167—We will tell each generation (Psalm 78)

compassion: *see: 'mercy', 'love'*

97—Lord Jesus, for my sake you come

conflict

49—God is our fortress and our rock (UK)

50—God is our fortress and our rock (USA)

courage

104—May the Lord God hear you pray (Psalm 20)

105—My faithful shepherd is the Lord (Psalm 23)

164—We lift our hearts up to the Lord

creation

4—Angels, praise him
32—Creator of the stars of light
41—Give thanks to God, for he is good (Psalm 136)
44—Glory and honor (canticle)
52—God of light and life's creation
56—God the Father caused to be (affirmation)
57—God the Father of creation (affirmation)
71—I believe in God the Father (affirmation)
81—In majesty and splendor (Psalm 104)
111—O bless the Lord, my soul (Psalm 104)
122—O Lord, our Lord, how wonderful (Psalm 8)
123—O Lord, our Lord, your beauty fills (Psalm 8)
130—Praise him, praise him, praise him (Psalm 148)
136—Roar the waves
144—Sing to the Lord (Psalm 96)
151—The God of heaven thunders (Psalm 29)
153—The majesty of mountains (Psalm 104)
159—To your praise, O God almighty
181—Who can bind the raging sea
183—You laid the foundations of earth (Psalm 102)

Cross: *see 'Passion tide'*

99—Lord of love
56—God the Father caused to be (affirmation)
71—I believe in God the Father (affirmation)
89—Jesus, redeemer, Mary's child
97—Lord Jesus, for my sake you come
112—O Christ of all the ages
131—Praise the Father, God of justice
152—The hands of Christ

danger

7—Be gracious to me, Lord (Psalm 57)
27—Come, join to praise our God (Psalm 89)
65—Hear me, O Lord (Psalm 86)
73—I love you, Lord, my rock (Psalm 18)
167—We will tell each generation (Psalm 78)
179—When the waters cover me (Psalm 69)

death, dying

81—In majesty and splendor (Psalm 104)
111—O bless the Lord, my soul (Psalm 104)
115—O God beyond all praising
117—O gracious Lord, be near me (Psalm 6)
124—O Lord, the God who saves me (Psalm 88)
125—O people, listen (Psalm 49)
149—Surely God the Lord is good (Psalm 73)

174—When Jesus Christ

dedication
52—God of light and life's creation
88—Jesus, redeemer, come
161—We give God thanks for those who knew
165—We share a new day's dawn
166—We thank you, God (communion)

demons
175—When Jesus walked upon this earth

despair
72—I cried out for heaven to hear me (Psalm 77)
179—When the waters cover me (Psalm 69)

devotion
97—Lord Jesus, for my sake you come
98—Lord Jesus, let these eyes of mine

disappointment
179—When the waters cover me (Psalm 69)

discipline
119—O Lord, come quickly when I call (Psalm 141)

dying
117—O gracious Lord, be near me (Psalm 6)

Easter
5—As we walk along beside you (Communion, Emmaus)
30—Comes Mary to the grave
112—O Christ of all the ages

empathy
33—Down from the height (canticle)

environment: *see 'creation', 'responsibility'*
122—O Lord, our Lord, how wonderful (Psalm 8)

Epiphany
110—O bless the God of Israel (canticle)
118—O Jesus, my Lord
144—Sing to the Lord (Psalm 96)
146—Soldiers marching
174—When Jesus Christ

Eucharist: *see 'Communion'*

evening
82—In majesty and splendor
95—Like a mighty river
108—Now evening comes (canticle)

310

119—O Lord, come quickly when I call

evil
49—God is our fortress and our rock (UK)
50—God is our fortress and our rock (USA)
62—He lives in us, the Christ of God
75—I will give thanks to the Lord most high (Psalm 7)
138—Save me, O God, hear my prayer (Psalm 54)
160—We are a land/world divided (Psalm 60)
175—When Jesus walked upon this earth
176—When my bitter foes surround

faith
35—Fling wide the gates (Psalm 24)
88—Jesus, redeemer, come
134—Ring out the bells and let the people

faithfulness, ours and God's
74—I praise you, Lord, with all my heart (Psalm 9)
77—I'll praise you, Lord (Psalm 138)
183—You laid the foundations of earth (Psalm 102)

family: *see also 'home', 'children'*
68—How blessed are those who live by faith (Psalm 112)

fear
63—Heal me, hands of Christ
64—Heal me, hands of Jesus
105—My faithful shepherd is the Lord (Psalm 23)
173—When I'm afraid (Psalm 56)
179—When the waters cover me (Psalm 69)

fellowship
53—God our Father, bless your people

flowers
3—All who are thirsty
95—Like a mighty river flowing

forgiveness
13—Born of the water
42—Given by grace (Communion)
62—He lives in us, the Christ of God
63—Heal me, hands of Christ
64—Heal me, hands of Jesus
88—Jesus, redeemer, come
95—Like a mighty river flowing
126—O praise the Lord, the mighty God (canticle)
150—The brightness of God's glory
152—The hands of Christ

311

freedom: *see 'release'*
106—No sorrow, no mourning, no crying

friends, friendship
95—Like a mighty river flowing
100—Lord, you are love
108—Now evening comes
179—When the waters cover me (Psalm 69)

future: *see also 'New Year', 'time'*
115—O God beyond all praising

generations: *see 'children', 'family'*
53—God our Father, bless your people
54—God save and bless our nation

gloria
45—Glory be to God in heaven (canticle)
66—Hear the skies around (Christmas)
149—Surely God the Lord is good (Psalm 73)

glory
44—Glory and honor (canticle)
45—Glory be to God in heaven (canticle)
55—God speaks—the Lord of all the earth (Psalm 50)
150—The brightness of God's glory
151—The God of heaven thunders (Psalm 29)

gospel
69—How shall they hear

grace
99—Lord of love
122—O Lord, our Lord, how wonderful (Psalm 8)
123—O Lord, our Lord, your beauty fills (Psalm 8)
180—When we walk with God (Psalm 1)

guidance
104—May the Lord God hear you pray (Psalm 20)
149—Surely God the Lord is good (Psalm 73)

guilt
63—Heal me, hands of Christ
64—Heal me, hands of Jesus
179—When the waters cover me (Psalm 69)

hands
98—Lord Jesus, let these eyes of mine
152—The hands of Christ

happiness
60—Happiness is simple trust (beatitudes)

68—How blessed are those who live by faith (Psalm 112)

harvest
81—In majesty and splendor (Psalm 104)

healing
63—Heal me, hands of Christ
128—One thing I know
161—We give God thanks for those who knew
175—When Jesus walked upon this earth

heaven
57—God the Father of creation (affirmation)
63—Heal me, hands of Christ
64—Heal me, hands of Jesus
89—Jesus, redeemer, Mary's child
125—O people, listen (Psalm 49)
134—Ring out the bells and let the people
149—Surely God the Lord is good (Psalm 73)

hills
95—Like a mighty river flowing

holiness
60—Happiness is simple trust (beatitudes)
144—Sing to the Lord (Psalm 96)
157—To lead a blameless life, O Lord (Psalm 26)

home: *see 'children'*
68—How blessed are those who live by faith (Psalm 112)

Holy Spirit: *see 'Spirit'*

hope
63—Heal me, hands of Christ
64—Heal me, hands of Jesus
73—I love you, Lord, my rock (Psalm 18)
86—Jesus, hope of every nation (canticle)
128—One thing I know

humble, the
47—Glory to the Lord of love (canticle)
103—Mary sang a song (canticle)

humility
33—Down from the height (canticle)
52—God of light and life's creation
60—Happiness is simple trust (beatitudes)
89—Jesus, redeemer, Mary's child
97—Lord Jesus, for my sake you come
129—Only the fool will say (Psalm 53)

pain

63—Heal me, hands of Christ
64—Heal me, hands of Jesus
108—Now evening comes
118—O Jesus, my Lord (Christmas)
161—We give God thanks
164—We lift our hearts up to the Lord

pardon

62—He lives in us, the Christ of God

Passion tide: *see 'Cross'*

33—Down from the height (canticle)
97—Lord Jesus, for my sake you come
112—O Christ of all the ages
142—The hands of Christ

patience

60—Happiness is simple trust (beatitudes)
137—Safe in the hands of God (Psalm 27)

peace

42—Given by grace (Communion)
45—Glory be to God in heaven (canticle)
58—God whose love we cannot measure (prayer)
63—Heal me, hands of Christ
64—Heal me, hands of Jesus
69—How shall they hear
77—I'll praise you, Lord (Psalm 138)
95—Like a mighty river flowing
106—No sorrow, no mourning, no crying
107—Not the grandeur of the mountains
129—Only the fool will say (Psalm 53)
131—Praise the Father, God of justice
156—To God's loving-kindness (benediction)
160—We are a land/world divided (Psalm 60)
164—We lift our hearts up to the Lord
174—When Jesus Christ
175—When Jesus walked upon this earth

penitence: *see also 'repentance'*

124—O Lord, the God who saves me (Psalm 88)
163—We have heard, O Lord our God (Psalm 44)

people

29—Come, worship God who is worthy (Psalm 95)
74—I praise you, Lord, with all my heart (Psalm 9)

persecution

60—Happiness is simple trust (beatitudes)

plans: *see also 'guidance'*
104—May the Lord God hear you pray (Psalm 20)

poor: *see also 'hungry'*
48—God is king—be warned, you mighty (Psalm 82)
60—Happiness is simple trust (beatitudes)
69—How shall they hear
103—Mary sang a song (canticle)
158—To those who rule our land (Psalm 72)

power
28—Come, sing praises to the Lord (Psalm 95)
48—God is king—be warned, you mighty (Psalm 82)
62—He lives in us, the Christ of God
72—I cried out for heaven to hear me (Psalm 77)
73—I love you, Lord, my rock (Psalm 18)
139—Savior Christ, in mercy come (canticle)

praise
14—Bring to the Lord a glad new song (Psalm 149, Psalm 150)
27—Come, join to praise our God (Psalm 89)
93—Lift up your hearts to the Lord (canticle)
111—O bless the Lord, my soul (Psalm 104)
128—One thing I know
130—Praise him, praise him, praise him (Psalm 148)
157—To lead a blameless life, O Lord (Psalm 26)
159—To your praise, O God almighty
173—When I'm afraid (Psalm 56)

prayer
58—God whose love we cannot measure (St. Boniface)
62—He lives in us, the Christ of God
73—I love you, Lord, my rock (Psalm 18)
95—Like a mighty river flowing
104—May the Lord God hear you pray (Psalm 20)
117—O gracious Lord, be near me (Psalm 6)
119—O Lord, come quickly when I call (Psalm 141)
120—O Lord, my rock, to you I cry (Psalm 120)
121—O Lord, my rock, to you I cry (Variant) (Psalm 120)
128—One thing I know
134—Ring out the bells and let the people
137—Safe in the hands of God (Psalm 27)
138—Save me, O God, hear my prayer (Psalm 54)
156—To God's loving-kindness (benediction)
157—To lead a blameless life, O Lord (Psalm 26)
165—We share a new day's dawn
172—When I lift up my voice (Psalm 142)

presence of God: *see 'walking with God'*
  39—From time beyond my memory (Psalm 71)
  54—God save and bless our nation
  180—When we walk with God (Psalm 1)

pride
  37—'From heaven above . .'
  54—God save and bless our nation
  80—In Christ there is no East or West (UK version)
  116—O God, we thank you that your name (Psalm 75)

proclamation: *see 'witness'*
  69—How shall they hear
  136—Roar the waves

promises, God's: *see 'faithfulness'*
  31—Commit your way to God the Lord (Psalm 37)
  105—My faithful shepherd is the Lord (Psalm 23)

protection: *see ''refuge', 'safety'*
  7—Be gracious to me, Lord (Psalm 57)
  65—Hear me, O Lord (Psalm 86)

Psalm versions
  6—Babylon, by the rivers of sorrow (137)
  7—Be gracious to me, Lord (57)
  14—Bring to the Lord a glad new song (149, 150)
  15—By flowing waters of Babylon (137)
  16—By rivers of sorrow we sat (137)
  22—Christ is king (110)
  27—Come, join to praise our God (89)
  28—Come, sing praises to the Lord (95)
  29—Come, worship God who is worthy (95)
  31—Commit your way to God the Lord (37)
  35—Fling wide the gates (24)
  39—From time beyond my memory (71)
  41—Give thanks to God, for he is good (thanks)
  48—God is king—be warned, you mighty (82)
  51—God is with the righteous (1)
  55—God speaks—the Lord of all the earth (50)
  59—God will arise (12)
  65—Hear me, O Lord (86)
  68—How blessed are those who live by faith (112)
  72—I cried out for heaven to hear me (77)
  73—I love you, Lord, my rock (18)
  74—I praise you, Lord, with all my heart (9)
  75—I will give thanks to the Lord most high (7)
  76—If we love the word of God (1)
  77—I'll praise you, Lord (138)

81—In majesty and splendor (104)
87—Jesus is our refuge (46)
93—Lift up your hearts to the Lord (98)
104—May the Lord God hear you pray (20)
105—My faithful shepherd is the Lord (23)
111—O bless the Lord, my soul (104)
116—O God, we thank you that your name (75)
117—O gracious Lord, be near me (6)
119—O Lord, come quickly when I call (141)
120—O Lord, my rock, to you I cry (120)
121—O Lord, my rock, to you I cry (Variant) (120)
122—O Lord, our Lord, how wonderful (8)
123—O Lord, our Lord, your beauty fills (8)
124—O Lord, the God who saves me (88)
125—O people, listen (49)
129—Only the fool will say (53)
130—Praise him, praise him, praise him (148)
137—Safe in the hands of God (27)
138—Save me, O God, hear my prayer (54)
144—Sing to the Lord (96)
148—Sovereign Lord, in all the earth (8)
149—Surely God the Lord is good (73)
151—The God of heaven thunders (29)
153—The majesty of mountains (104)
157—To lead a blameless life, O Lord (26)
158—To those who rule our land (72)
160—We are a land/world divided (60)
163—We have heard, O Lord our God (44)
167—We will tell each generation (78)
172—When I lift up my voice (142)
173—When I'm afraid (56)
176—When my bitter foes surround (43)
179—When the waters cover me (69)
180—When we walk with God (1)
183—You laid the foundations of earth (102)

punishment
75—I will give thanks to the Lord most high (Psalm 7)

ransom: *see also 'atonement', 'redemption'*
44—Glory and honor (canticle)

rebellion: *see 'obedience'*
167—We will tell each generation (Psalm 78)

reconciliation
80, 81—In Christ there is no East or West
89—Jesus, Redeemer
152—The hands of Christ

redeemer, redemption
32—Creator of the stars of light
44—Glory and honor (canticle)
57—God the Father of creation (affirmation)
71—I believe in God the Father (affirmation)
88—Jesus, redeemer, come
99—Lord of love
89—Jesus, Redeemer
114—O come, our world's Redeemer
126—O praise the Lord, the mighty God (canticle)

refreshment, renewal
3—All who are thirsty (Communion)
51—God is with the righteous (Psalm 1)
76—If we love the word of God (Psalm 1)
87—Jesus is our refuge (Psalm 46)
105—My faithful shepherd is the Lord (Psalm 23)
106—No sorrow, no mourning, no crying

refuge: *see also 'safety', 'security'*
137—Safe in the hands of God (Psalm 27)
172—When I lift up my voice (Psalm 142)

release: *see also 'freedom'*
10—Blest be the God of Israel (canticle)
41—Give thanks to God, for he is good (Psalm 136)
42—Given by grace (Communion)
69—How shall they hear
139—Savior Christ, in mercy come (canticle)
175—When Jesus walked upon this earth

repentance: *see also 'penitence'*
69—How shall they hear
179—When the waters cover me (Psalm 69)

rescue: *see also 'salvation'*
75—I will give thanks to the Lord most high (Psalm 7)
87—Jesus is our refuge (Psalm 46)

responsibility
148—Sovereign Lord, in all the earth (Psalm 8)

resurrection, Jesus' and ours
30—Comes Mary to the grave (Easter)
71—I believe in God the Father (affirmation)
83—In the streets of every city
89—Jesus, redeemer, Mary's child
131—Praise the Father, God of justice
152—The hands of Christ

righteousness
27—Come, join to praise our God (Psalm 89)
48—God is king—be warned, you mighty (Psalm 82)
51—God is with the righteous (Psalm 1)
157—To lead a blameless life, O Lord (Psalm 26)

river
95—Like a mighty river flowing

rulers: *see also 'leaders'*
14—Bring to the Lord a glad new song (Psalm 149, Psalm 150)
48—God is king—be warned, you mighty (Psalm 82)
158—To those who rule our land (Psalm 72)

safety: *see also 'refuge', 'security'*
137—Safe in the hands of God (Psalm 27)

saints
130—Praise him, praise him, praise him (Psalm 148)
159—To your praise, O God almighty

salvation: *see also 'redemption'*
35—Fling wide the gates (Psalm 24)
129—Only the fool will say (Psalm 53)
150—The brightness of God's glory

Savior of the World
139—Savior Christ, in mercy come (canticle)

sea
27—Come, join to praise our God (Psalm 89)
95—Like a mighty river flowing
107—Not the grandeur of the mountains
111—O bless the Lord, my soul (Psalm 104)
136—Roar the waves

security
137—Safe in the hands of God (Psalm 27)
173—When I'm afraid (Psalm 56)

service
53—God our Father, bless your people
98—Lord Jesus, let these eyes of mine
165—We share a new day's dawn

shepherd
72—I cried out for heaven to hear me (Psalm 77)
105—My faithful shepherd is the Lord (Psalm 23)
120—O Lord, my rock, to you I cry (Psalm 120)
121—O Lord, my rock, to you I cry (Variant) (Psalm 120)

sign

tears: *see also 'sorrow', 'despair'*
   60—Happiness is simple trust (beatitudes)
   179—When the waters cover me (Psalm 69)

temptation
   62—He lives in us, the Christ of God
   112—O Christ of all the ages
   150—The brightness of God's glory

thanksgiving
   3—All who are thirsty, come to the Lord
   29—Come, worship God
   41—Give thanks to God
   58—God whose love we cannot measure (prayer)
   75—I will give thanks to the Lord most high (Psalm 7)
   105—O God beyond all praising

time: *see also 'New Year'*
   39—From time beyond my memory (Psalm 71)
   47—Glory to the Lord of love (canticle)
   57—God the Father of creation (affirmation)
   81—In majesty and splendor (Psalm 104)
   112—O Christ of all the ages
   150—The brightness of God's glory

tiredness: *see also 'sleep'*
   149—Surely God the Lord is good (Psalm 73)

tongue
   59—God will arise
   69—How shall they hear the word of God
   98—Lord Jesus, let these eyes
   119—O Lord, come quickly when I call (Psalm 141)

Trinity
   53—God our Father, bless your people
   56—God the Father caused to be (affirmation)
   57—God the Father of creation (affirmation)
   131—Praise the Father, God of justice
   136—Roar the waves (in creation)

trouble
   7—Be gracious to me, Lord (Psalm 57)
   117—O gracious Lord, be near me (Psalm 6)
   124—O Lord, the God who saves me (Psalm 88)
   172—When I lift up my voice (Psalm 142)

trust
   29—Come, worship God who is worthy (Psalm 95)
   31—Commit your way to God the Lord (Psalm 37)

51—God is with the righteous (Psalm 1)
59—God will arise (Psalm 12)
74—I praise you, Lord, with all my heart (Psalm 9)
116—O God, we thank you that your name (Psalm 75)
176—When my bitter foes surround (Psalm 43)
180—When we walk with God (Psalm 1)

wisdom

44—Glory and honor (canticle)
125—O people, listen (Psalm 49)
129—Only the fool will say (Psalm 53)
139—Savior Christ, in mercy come (canticle)
181—Who can bind the raging sea

witness

77—I'll praise you, Lord (Psalm 138)
83—In the streets of every city
98—Lord Jesus, let these eyes of mine
99—Lord of love
166—We thank you, God (communion)

word

31—Commit your way to God the Lord (Psalm 37)
59—God will arise (Psalm 12)
76—If we love the word of God (Psalm 1)
130—Praise him, praise him, praise him (Psalm 148)
165—We share a new day's dawn

worship

28—Come, sing praises to the Lord (Psalm 95)
29—Come, worship God who is worthy (Psalm 95)
55—God speaks—the Lord of all the earth (Psalm 50)
65—Hear me, O Lord (Psalm 86)
77—I'll praise you, Lord (Psalm 138)
134—Ring out the bells and let the people
144—Sing to the Lord (Psalm 96)
151—The God of heaven thunders (Psalm 29)
159—To your praise, O God almighty

youth: *see 'children'*
39—From time beyond my memory (Psalm 71)

Metrical Index of Hymns and Songs

5.11.6.6.7.11.
  17   Child in a stable

5.4.5.4.D.
  3   All who are thirsty

5.5.7.7.D.
  13   Born of the water

5.5.8.D.
  12   Born as a stranger

5.5.9.5.5.8.
  44   Glory and honor

5.6.8.6.
  63   Heal me, hands of Christ

6.6.11.D.
  11   Blow upon the trumpet

6.6.6.5.D.
  154   The story has broken

6.6.6.6.6.5.5.6.6.
  142   Shout aloud, girls and boys

6.6.6.6.6.7.7.6.
  87   Jesus is our refuge

6.6.6.6.Ref.
  122   O Lord, our Lord, how wonderful

6.6.8.8.6.
  158   To those who rule our land

6.6.8.D.
  113   O come, Christians, wonder

6.7.7.11.
  30   Comes Mary to the grave

7.3.3.7.7.
  141   Shepherds, wake to news of joy

7.3.7.8.8.7.7.
  90   Jesus, savior, holy child

7.4.7.4.
  25   Come and praise the Lord our king

7.4.7.7.7.4.
  179   When the waters cover me

7.6.7.6.

7.7.8.7.D.
  82   In the darkness of the night

7.8.7.7.
  19   Child of heaven, born on earth

7.8.8.8.
  60   Happiness is simple trust

8.3.8.8.
  1   A child is born in Bethlehem

8.4.4.4.
  34   Fear not, for I bring all people

8.4.8.4.8.8.8.4.
  26   Come and sing the Christmas story

8.4.8.8.5.7.
  175   When Jesus walked upon this earth

8.5.8.5.
  53   God our Father, bless your people

8.5.8.5.8.7.
  46   Glory in the highest heaven

8.6.8.6.8.8.
  69   How shall they hear

8.6.8.8.6.
  121   O Lord, my rock, to you I cry (Variant)

8.7.7.8.
  180   When we walk with God

8.7.8.7.
  9   Bethlehem, what greater city
  22   Christ is king
  57   God the Father of creation
  71   I believe in God the Father
  86   Jesus, hope of every nation
  119   O Lord, come quickly when I call
  131   Praise the Father, God of justice
  167   We will tell each generation
  169   Welcome, Jesus, Child of Mary

8.7.8.7. iambic
  2   All heaven rings with joyful songs

8.7.8.7.6.5.6.6.7.
  50   God is our fortress and our rock (USA)

8.7.8.7.6.6.6.6.7.

49   God is our fortress and our rock (UK)

8.7.8.7.7.7.
52   God of light and life's creation

8.7.8.7.8.6.
21   Christ is born within a stable

8.7.8.7.8.7.
83   In the streets of every city
136   Roar the waves

8.7.8.7.D.
24   Come and hear the joyful singing
27   Come, join to praise our God
45   Glory be to God in heaven
48   God is king—be warned, you mighty
58   God whose love we cannot measure
107   Not the grandeur of the mountains
159   To your praise, O God almighty

8.7.8.8.7.
164   We lift our hearts up to the Lord

8.8.7.
145   Sleep, Lord Jesus

8.8.8.11.
5   As we walk along beside you

8.8.8.7.
18   Child of gladness, child of sorrow
41   Give thanks to God, for he is good
95   Like a mighty river flowing

8.8.8.8.4.
152   The hands of Christ

8.8.8.8.8.
165   We share a new day's dawn

9.7.8.5.
173   When I'm afraid

9.8.5.4.8.
155   There's a bright sky over Bethlehem

9.8.9.8.
15   By flowing waters of Babylon
72   I cried out for heaven to hear me
137   Safe in the hands of God

9.8.9.9.

Val: INDEX.DOC.
February 27, 1995; 10:56 AM
Pages: 50; word count: 13100.
Revision: 28; last saved: 27/02/95.
Printed: 27/02/95; Created: 18/02/95.